# C Programming for the PIC Microcontroller

## Demystify Coding with Embedded Programming

Hubert Henry Ward

Apress®

*C Programming for the PIC Microcontroller: Demystify Coding with Embedded Programming*

Hubert Henry Ward
Lancashire, UK

ISBN-13 (pbk): 978-1-4842-5524-7     ISBN-13 (electronic): 978-1-4842-5525-4
https://doi.org/10.1007/978-1-4842-5525-4

Managing Director, Apress Media LLC: Welmoed Spahr
Acquisitions Editor: Natalie Pao
Development Editor: James Markham
Coordinating Editor: Jessica Vakili

Distributed to the book trade worldwide by Springer Science+Business Media New York, 233 Spring Street, 6th Floor, New York, NY 10013. Phone 1-800-SPRINGER, fax (201) 348-4505, e-mail orders-ny@springer-sbm.com, or visit www.springeronline.com. Apress Media, LLC is a California LLC and the sole member (owner) is Springer Science + Business Media Finance Inc (SSBM Finance Inc). SSBM Finance Inc is a **Delaware** corporation.

For information on translations, please e-mail rights@apress.com, or visit http://www.apress.com/rights-permissions.

Apress titles may be purchased in bulk for academic, corporate, or promotional use. eBook versions and licenses are also available for most titles. For more information, reference our Print and eBook Bulk Sales web page at http://www.apress.com/bulk-sales.

Any source code or other supplementary material referenced by the author in this book is available to readers on GitHub via the book's product page, located at www.apress.com/978-1-4842-5524-7. For more detailed information, please visit http://www.apress.com/source-code.

Printed on acid-free paper

*Dedicated to my wife Ann*

# Table of Contents

# About the Author

**Hubert Henry Ward** has over 24 years of experience in teaching students at the Higher National Certificate and the Higher Diploma in Electrical and Electronic Engineering. Hubert has a 2.1 Honours Bachelor's Degree in Electrical & Electronic Engineering. Hubert has also worked as a college lecturer and consultant in embedded programming. His work has established his expertise in the assembler language and C, MPLABX, and designing electronic circuit and PCBs using ECAD software. Hubert was also the UK technical expert in Mechatronics for 3 years, training the UK team and taking them to enter in the Skills Olympics in Seoul 2001, resulting in one of the best outcomes to date for the United Kingdom in Mechatronics.

# About the Technical Reviewer

**Leigh Orme** is a graduate engineer at SSE plc in Greater Manchester, United Kingdom. He has an electrical and electronic engineering degree from Manchester Metropolitan University.

# Introduction

This book looks at programming a PIC microcontroller in C. We'll study the following aspects of programming the PIC:

1. Looking at some of the background to the program language for micros

2. Creating a project in the Microchip IDE MPLABX

3. Configuring the PIC

4. Setting up the oscillator using the internal oscillator block

5. Setting up some digital inputs and outputs

6. Simulating a simple program using the simulator in MPLABX

7. Creating a simple delay and a variable delay

8. Using the ADC to accommodate an analogue input to the PIC

9. Using an LCD in both 4-bit and 8-bit mode to display data

10. How to make a header file to save writing the same instructions again in every project.

11. Using arrays and controlling how you step through an array

# The Aim of the Book

The aim of this book is to introduce the reader to PIC microcontrollers and writing programs in 'C'. There is some background information starting with what a PIC is and some aspects of programming languages. It will then move onto what an IDE is and how to use MPLABX, one of the most common industrial IDEs. MPLABX is an IDE that is freely available from the Microchip web site. The 'C' compiler is their free compiler that again can be downloaded from their web site. Note that I use MPLABX version 5.2 and the XC8 compiler version 2.05 or 1.35. These can be downloaded from the archive section of their web site.

Then the text moves on to the exciting world of writing programs for microcontrollers. It is based around the range of microcontrollers, termed PIC micros, available from Microchip. It will show you how to write programs without buying any devices or equipment as you can use the MPLABX simulators that come free with the MPLABX IDE. If you have access to an ECAD package, such as PROTEUS or Tina, that has the ability to run 8-bit or 16-bit and so on micros, then it will show you how to use that software to run your programs, again without buying any equipment.

This book is based around the PIC18F4525 as it has the advantage of being a 40 pin dual in line package. This means it is quite easy for the hobbyist to create a practical circuit on vero board or even a small PCB.

My other books cover using the PIC to control a variety of DC motors such as simple DC motors using PWM to control the speed of the DC motor, stepper motors, and servo motors. I also have a short book looking at communications for the 18F4525. Apart from those books, I am writing another range of books on how to use a 32-bit PIC, but this is a surface mount device which makes it rather more difficult to build practical circuits. However, the 32-bit PICs have some very useful additions.

The PIC18F4525 is a very useful PIC with 5 ports giving us the use of 36 I/O. It has 4 timers and 3 external interrupt sources. It has a two-CCP module with the ability to provide two separate PWM outputs, and it has full bridge drive capabilities. There are more functions available, and they all make the PIC18F4525 a very useful microcontroller.

# The Objectives of the Book

After reading this book, you should be able to do the following:

- Write PIC programs in C

- Use the main features of the MPLABX IDE

- Interface the PIC to the real world

- Design and create useful programs based around the PIC18F4525

- Enjoy delving into the exciting world of embedded programming

I hope you enjoy reading this book and find it very useful. I firmly believe that programmers should not just put together blocks of code, which perform the functions they want, to create a program. To be a good programmer, with the versatility to alter their programs to cope with the wide variety of microcontrollers and their different oscillator choices, you need to know how the code works. In my many years of teaching this subject, I have often been told that to create a 1-second delay, you simply write the instruction delay (1000). Well, that only works for a certain oscillator frequency and timer setting. To be able to create a delay using any oscillator, you need to understand how your timer counts and at what frequency it counts. Armed with that sort of deeper understanding, you will be a better programmer.

This book is aimed at giving you the full understanding of the fundamental aspects of the microcontroller and how it works. Then, with a deeper understanding of how the different control registers control the micro, you will become a programmer who will, with experience, fully control your device and not rely on bits of code, which you don't understand, doing the programming for you. It is essential that we have programmers who have this deep appreciation of their microcontrollers, and I hope that after reading this book, you are on your way to becoming one of those programmers.

# The Prerequites for the Book

There are none really, but if you understand 'C' programming, it would be useful. Also, if you understand the binary and hexadecimal number systems, it would be an advantage, but there is a section in the Appendix that will help you with that.

# CHAPTER 1

# Introduction

This chapter covers some of the fundamentals of what a microprocessor-based system is and how a microcontroller is different. It then covers the historic development of the 'C' programming language for PIC controllers.

After reading this chapter, you should appreciate how the micro sees your instructions and understand the terms machine code, assembler, compiler, and linker.

## Programmable Industrial Controllers

Programmable Industrial Controllers (PICs) is really just a trademark for the microcontrollers produced by Microchip, or so I have been led to believe. Some say it stands for Programmable Industrial Controllers, or Programmable Intelligent Controller, or Programmable Interface Controller. However, the term PIC is used by Microchip to cover an extremely wide range of microcontrollers produced by them. I will simply refer to the microcontroller as the PIC.

Each PIC will have all the components of a microprocessor-based system as shown in Figure 1-1, such as

- A microprocessor

- ROM, RAM

- An I/O chip

- The associated address, data, and control buses

© Hubert Henry Ward 2020
H. H. Ward, *C Programming for the PIC Microcontroller*,
https://doi.org/10.1007/978-1-4842-5525-4_1

However, all these parts are all on a single chip, not several as with older microprocessor-based systems. This means it is really a single-chip computer.

As well as all that, the PIC has much more circuitry on the single chip. This extra circuitry is used to make it into a control system with a micro at the heart of it. The extra circuit may include an ADC, opamp circuits for compare and capture, a PWM module, and a UART module. These extra circuits may not be on all PICs as PICs vary in their makeup for different applications.

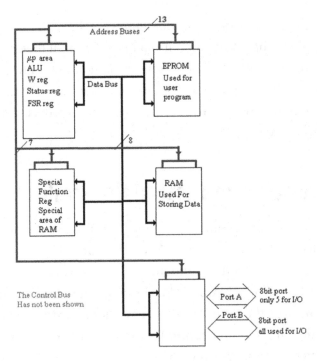

***Figure 1-1.*** *The Basic Microprocessor System*

One more thing before we move on is that the PIC is a RISC chip as opposed to a CISC chip. RISC stands for reduced instruction set chip, whereas CISC stands for complex instruction set chip. Indeed, the instruction set for PIC micros ranges from 35 to 75 core instructions. However, the 18F4525 has an extended instruction set at your disposal. The Intel processor, which is a CISC chip, uses hundreds of instructions. So the PIC is pretty efficient.

# Programming Languages

There is a wide variety of programming languages for microprocessor-based systems. However, all microprocessors only understand voltage levels, ideally 5V and 0V. These two voltage levels are how all microprocessors understand logic which has only two states which are "yes or no," 5V or 0V, and now 3.3v and 0v as with the 32-bit PICs.

It is because of this that the binary number system is commonly used in microprocessor-based systems. This is because binary only has two discrete digits '1' and '0'.

Consider the following binary number:

10101001

This really represents

5v0v5v0v5v0v0v5v

The 5v and 0v is really the only language that all microprocessors understand. However, we can easily use binary to represent the 5v and 0v as '1' and '0'. So writing in binary is easier than writing 5v and 0v.

# Machine Code

This then is the birth of "machine code," the most basic programming language termed low level as it is at the level that the micro understands.

Now consider the following:

A9

This is a hexadecimal representation of the 8 binary bits 10101001. It is used to enable programmers to represent binary numbers in a less complicated manner to avoid mistakes, as its very easy to write a '0' instead of a '1'. However, the early programmers actually wrote their

3

programs in the binary machine code to make them faster. There is a section in the Appendix that covers the binary and hexadecimal number systems which is something you need to understand. See Appendix 7.

Now consider the following:

> LDA#
>
> This is actually termed "mnemonics" which stands for an alphanumeric code used to represent the instruction.
>
> The mnemonic LDA# represents the instruction

LoaD the Accumulator immediately with the number that follows:

> 'LD' for load, 'A' for accumulator, and '#' for immediately.

It is fairly obvious that we, as humans, can learn to understand the mnemonics quicker than hexadecimal or the binary of the machine code. However, the microprocessor does not understand these mnemonics. Somehow the mnemonics has to be converted to the machine code.

Consider the following:

LDA#      A9    10101001

The first column is the code or mnemonics; the next two columns are the conversion to the machine code via hexadecimal and then to binary. Every instruction in the micros instruction set has its hexadecimal or binary equivalent. With the EMMA systems, the students actually converted the mnemonics code to the machine code, but this is very time-consuming.

The act of converting the mnemonics to machine code is called "compiling," and with the EMMAs, we get the students to compile the mnemonics. In real programming, we use a program called a compiler to do this.

# Assembler Language

Different micros use different mnemonics to represent the instructions in their instruction set. All these different mnemonics are now collectively termed assembler language. There are different ones for different systems such as TASAM for TINA with the EMMAs, MASAM for Microsoft used in DOS programs, and MPLAB assembler from Microchip.

When using assembler language, all instructions have two parts:

- The OPCODE. This is the part that describes the operation (i.e., LDA Load The Accumulator).

- The OPERAND. Where the micro gets the data to be used in the operation (i.e., '#').

This means that the data is what follows immediately next in the micros memory.

As this book is based on the C programming language, there is no real need for the reader to understand the assembly language, but it is important to realize that all program languages, even visual basic, have to be converted to the machine code before being loaded into the micro. This process is called compiling, and it usually involves converting the program instructions into assembler before going into machine code.

# C Programming Language

C and now C++ are generic programming languages that many programmers now study. As this has meant that there are a lot of engineers who can program in this language, then Microchip, the manufactures of PICs, have produced 'C' compilers that can be used to convert a 'C' program into the machine code for their PICs. Indeed, as the number of programmers who write in assembler have reduced and the number of 'C' programmers have increased, Microchip has stopped writing assembler compilers for their more advanced PICs such as the 32-bit PICs. Also, I believe that Siemens is now moving toward programming their PLCs in 'C'.

The more modern languages such as Python and C# have their roots in 'C'.

# Different Programming Languages

Table 1-1 shows some of the more common programming languages.

***Table 1-1.*** *Some Common Programming Languages*

| Example Language |
| --- |
| Machine code (binary 1s and 0s) |
| Assembly Language |
| Cobol |
| Fortran |
| C, Pascal |
| Ada 83 |
| C++, |
| C# |
| Python |
| Basic |
| Visual Basic |

# The IDE

The term IDE stands for integrated development environment. It is actually a collection of the different programs needed to write program instructions in our chosen language. Then convert them to the actual machine code that the micro understands, and also link together any bits of program we may want to use.

The programs we need in the IDE are

- A text editor to write the instructions for the program. Note: The simple text editor "Notepad" could be used, but the text editor in MPLABX is by far a more advanced text editor.

- A compiler to change the instructions into a format the micro can understand.

- A linker to combine any files the programmer wants to use.

- A driver that will allow the programming tool used to load the program into the micro.

- A variety of simulation tools to allow the programmer to test aspects of the program.

- A variety of debug tools to allow the programmer to test the program live within the micro.

All these are in the IDE we choose; Microsoft has Visual Studio, Microchip has MPLABX, and Freescale uses CodeWarrior. Note that CODEBLOCK is an IDE for writing generic 'C' programs that will run on your PC. As this book is based on the PIC micro, it will concentrate on MPLABX. MPLABX has an improved text editor to give the text different color codes when we save the file as a .asm or .c for c program file such as light blue for keywords, light gray for comments, and so on.

There are some other organization programs within MPLABX such as the ability to write to the configuration registers for the PIC. There is also the ability to simulate your programs within the IDE. All this makes MPLABX a useful tool for programming PICs.

There is also a program called MCC Microchip Code Configurator. This will actually produce a lot of the code you need, to use various aspects of the PIC, for you. However, I firmly believe that you should produce the code you use yourself so that you fully understand the code you use. I will not cover the use of the MCC. Also, Microchip has not written the MCC for all their PICs, and the 18F4525 is one they have missed so far.

Really when asked who the programmer is, you should be able to say that you are and not the MCC. When you take the time to study how to write your own code, you will find it is not as hard as you first thought. Also, you will get a better self-reward if you write it all yourself.

The only aspect of the programs that I let Microchip do for me is to write the code configuration bits that set up the PIC. This is only because it is so simple to do this and it covers all the #pragma statements.

## Summary

This chapter has given you some background information about microcontrollers. It has introduced some of the terms and given you an explanation of what they mean such as

- PIC

- IDE

The next chapter will take you through creating a project in MPLABX the IDE from Microchip. It will also allow you to produce your first PIC program.

# CHAPTER 2

# Our First Program

After reading this chapter, you should be able to create a project and write a program that uses inputs from switches and turns on outputs. We are going to start off by writing a program that will make the PIC wait until a switch connected to bit 0 of PORTA goes high. It will then light an LED on bit 0 of PORTB. The PIC will then wait until a second switch, connected this time to bit 1 of PORTA, goes high. When this happens, the LED on bit 0 of PORTB will be turned off. Note that both switches will be single momentary switches, that is, they will stay high only when they are pressed; when they are released, their logic will go low.

## The PORTS of the PIC

Before I go any further, I think I should explain that the PORTS are the actual physical connections that the PIC uses to connect to the outside world. Note that the micros have used the analogy of the real ports, such as the Port of London or the Port of Liverpool, which actually connect the country to the outside world taking goods in for the country and sending goods out of the country.

These PORTS connect internally to registers inside the PIC. The registers are merely a collection of individual cells which we call bits. In the 18f4525 there are 8 cells or bits connected together to form a register. This is because the 18f4525 is an 8-bit micro. These bits are numbered from right to left as bit 0, bit 1, bit 2, bit 3, bit 4, bit 5, bit 6, and bit 7. This is shown in Figure 2-1.

© Hubert Henry Ward 2020
H. H. Ward, *C Programming for the PIC Microcontroller*,
https://doi.org/10.1007/978-1-4842-5525-4_2

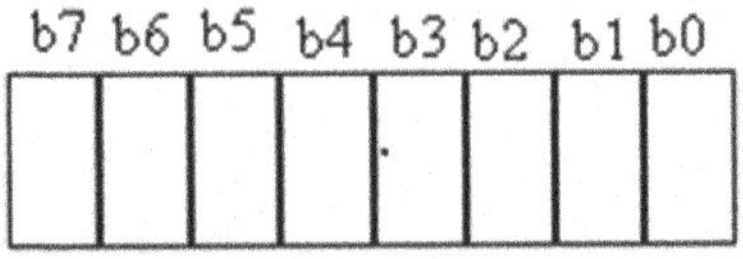

***Figure 2-1.*** *An 8-Bit Register*

The bit 0 is sometimes referred to as the LSB or least significant bit, as this represents the units column or the ones column; whereas the bit7 is the MSB, most significant bit, as this represents the 128 column. Note that a 32-bit micro will have 32 bits in their registers and PORTS.

# Good Programming Practice

All programs should be planned. The programmer should not just start writing code in the IDE. A good programmer should write an algorithm then construct a flowchart then write the program listing.

# The Algorithm

This is really simply putting your thoughts, of how you are going to get the PIC to do what is asked of it, down on paper. The purpose is to focus your mind on how to complete the task. It will also allow you to choose the right PIC for the job. The algorithm should cover at least the following:

- You should explain the sequence of events you want to control.

- You should then identify all the input and output devices you will need.

- You should then create an allocation list for the control and identify any special inputs or outputs or controls you will need, such as analogue inputs, PWM outputs, and any timers.

# The Flowchart

This is a diagram using standard symbols to show how the program will flow through the instructions and so complete the task.

Flowcharts are diagrams that show how any process flow through its constituent parts. They are very useful diagrams for designing computer programs. All flowcharts use five basic symbols; there are more, but the five most common symbols are shown in Figure 2-2.

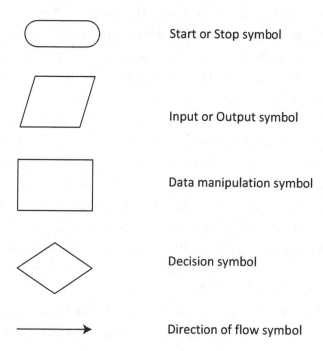

Start or Stop symbol

Input or Output symbol

Data manipulation symbol

Decision symbol

Direction of flow symbol

*Figure 2-2.* *The Main Flowchart Symbols*

# The Program Listing

This is a list of the actual instructions written in your chosen language. If you have constructed your flowchart correctly, then each block in your flowchart will produce the correct lines of coding in your program listing.

# Using MPLABX IDE

Before we go too far into the depths of MPLABX, I will discuss the use of MCC and MPLAB Harmony. Microchip has realized that there are many aspects of writing programs for the PIC that have to be carried out within every program. Therefore, they give you the facility to use their code-generating programs to write the code for you. MCC, MPLABX Code Configurator, is the program that does this for you. MPLAB Harmony does this for the 32-bit micros. Wow, isn't that great? Well yes and no. Using MCC creates a myriad of files and functions that are not easy to understand. If you write all the code for your program yourself, then you know where all the bits are and you understand how they work. Also this book teaches you how to use the datasheet to help write the instructions. You will learn how the PIC actually works and how it uses the simple logic '1's and '0's to control how it works. I firmly believe it is important for you, as the programmer, to understand what you are controlling and how your program instructions actually control it. If you use MCC straight off, then you risk losing this understanding and who the programmer is, you or Microchip. If you write all your own code, then you are the programmer.

MPLABX is the new IDE from Microchip. It is written in Java, and it has many improvements from the previous MPLAB. The book is written around using MPLABX version 5.2.

The text is based around using the PIC18f4525, but it can easily be adapted for any PIC micro. The 18F4525 PIC is a very versatile PIC in that it has

- 36 I/O

- 13 ADC channels

- 2 CCP modules as well as a UART and SPI

It has 48 kbytes of program memory as well as internal EEPROM.

All this makes this PIC a very versatile PIC to use. Also, the fact that it is available in a dual in-line 40pin device means that you can easily make a prototype board based around this PIC.

# Creating the Project in MPLABX

It is noted that Microchip is forever bringing out new versions of their IDE. However, the basics do not really change, and if you learn how to use one version of the IDE, you will very quickly grasp how to move onto the new version. This book is based around version 5.2 which can be downloaded from the Microchip web site.

After installing the software and opening the program by clicking on the ICON 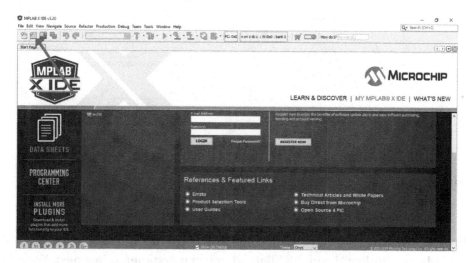, you will be presented with a screen that looks like that in Figure 2-3.

*Figure 2-3.* *The Opening Screen for MPLABX*

We need to create a project where all files for the task will be stored; these will include, among others, the asm or 'c' file that we will write and

13

more importantly the hex file that the compiler in MPLABX will create. It is this hex file that will be loaded into the PIC to make the PIC run our program.

To create a new project, click the mouse on the second symbol, the orange square with the small green cross, in the menu bar, as shown in Figure 2-3. Alternatively, you could select file from the menu bar, and then select "New Project," the top option from the dropdown menu that appears. The new project window will open as shown in Figure 2-4.

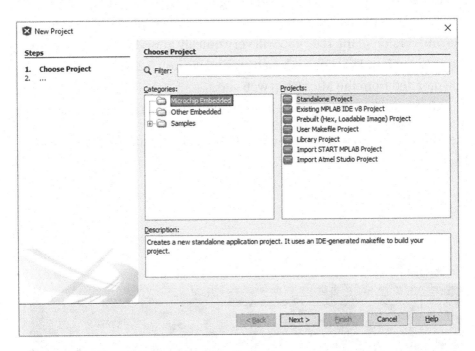

***Figure 2-4.*** *The New Project Window*

Click the mouse on the selection "Microchip Embedded" "Standalone Project" if it is not the default selection. If the "Microchip Embedded" "Standalone Project" is not highlighted, select it first then select next. You will now be presented with a window that looks similar to that shown in Figure 2-5.

14

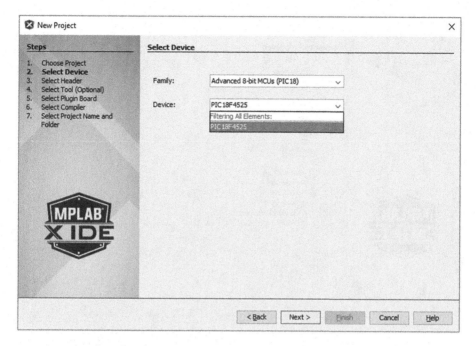

**Figure 2-5.** *Select Device Window*

We can now choose which PIC we will actually use. Alongside the "Family" window, click on the arrow, and select the Advanced 8-bit MCUs (PIC18) as shown earlier. Then alongside the "Device" window, click the arrow, and select the PIC18f4525 device as shown. Note that you could type the PIC number into the device box and the program will move the window down to the relevant PIC.

Once you are happy with your selection, click Next to move onto the next window as shown in Figure 2-6.

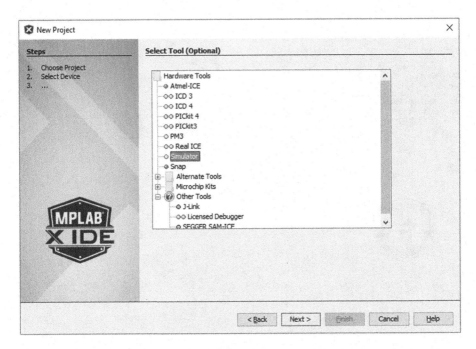

***Figure 2-6.*** *The Select Tool Window*

From within this window, the programmer can select the type of tool they want to use to download the program to the PIC and also debug and run the program. Normally we would be using the ICD 3, but as this is the first use of this software, we will use the IDE's simulation tool to examine the program as it runs. Therefore, select the Simulator option as previously shown.

Click Next to confirm the selection and move on to the next screen. This is shown in Figure 2-7.

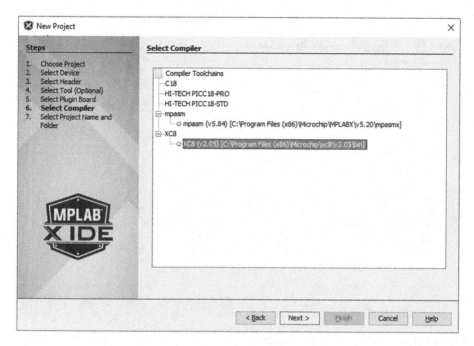

***Figure 2-7.*** *The Select Compiler Window*

This window shows what compilers have been installed on your system. Assuming you have a suitable XC8 compiler, you should be able to select it as shown in Figure 2-7. Once you have selected it, click Next, and the window shown in Figure 2-8 is presented.

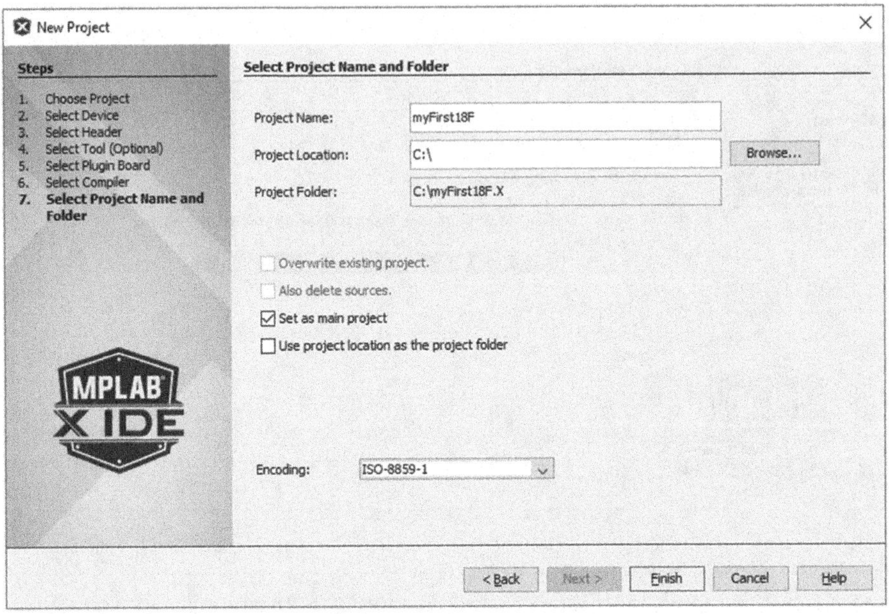

**Figure 2-8.** *Naming the Project*

This window is where you give a name for your project and decide where you want to save it. Make sure you know where you are saving your project, and give it the name "myFirst18F" as shown in Figure 2-8.

Note that I will use the method of using camelFont, to write any labels. This allows the programmer to write multiple words as one word. The first letter of the complete word is in lower case, but the first letter of all subsequent words is in capitals as in "myFirst18F".

Now click Finish and the project will be created. You will now be presented with the main window as shown in Figure 2-9.

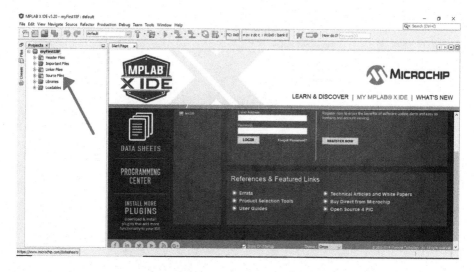

**Figure 2-9.** *The Completed Project*

We now need to add the text document that will contain all the 'C' instructions for the program. This will be the source file, and so we need to right click the mouse on the item source files in the project tree on the left-hand side. Now click the mouse on New, and then select **main.c** from the pop-out window that appears.

Having selected the **main.c** from the pop-out window, the following window shown in Figure 2-10 appears.

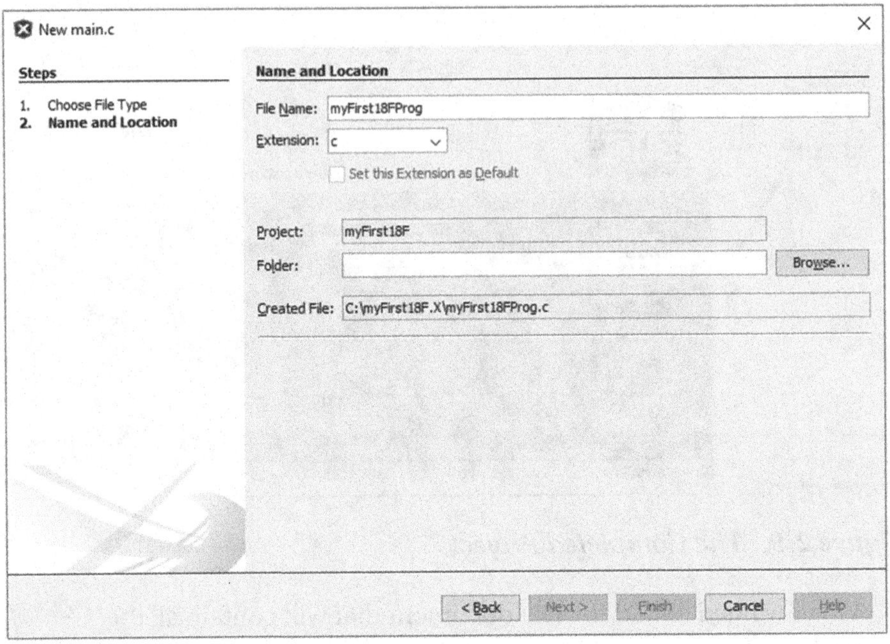

**Figure 2-10.** *The New Empty File Window*

Give the file the name myFirst18FProg and click on Finish. Note that the extension must be, as shown, '.c' to make it a 'C' program file.

Now the main editing window will appear as shown in Figure 2-11.

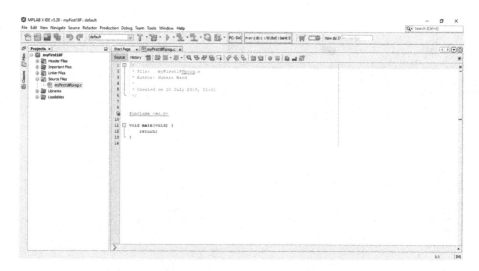

**Figure 2-11.** *The Editing Window*

It is in this screen that you will type all the instructions for your program.

The software has already inserted some comments from lines 1 to 6. This is because the software uses intelli-sense which is like predictive text on your phone. This software also automatically has added an "include" directive on line 9, and it has included the main loop between lines 11 and 13. More will be said about these later.

If the line numbers are not shown in the text editor and you would like to see them, as I do, then simply click on the word "View" from the main menu bar. Then tick the box to "Show Line Numbers" that appears on the fly-out menu, or un-tick it depending upon your preference. However, from experience I think it is useful to have line numbers showing as it helps with finding any errors in your coding.

We can change some of the fonts if you so wish by selecting the word "Options" from the drop-down menu that appears when you select the "Tools" choice on the main menu bar. You will get the window as shown in Figure 2-12.

**Figure 2-12.** *Changing the Comments Font*

Once you are happy with your choice, click OK. I have selected the Fonts & Colors, then changed the color of the comments to magenta.

You have now created your first project in MPLABX. You should practice the process of creating a project so that you are comfortable with the process. It will take some time but it is definitely worth it. Don't just modify an old project.

# The First Program Turning On and Off an Output

Now we are ready to get down to the real part of this process, writing the code for the program.

If you have never written a 'C' program, then there are some things you may need to read through at this point.

# The Main Aspects of a 'C' Program

The 'C' programming language is a generic language in that it can be applied to many different environments such as DOS, Windows Applications, and now microcontrollers. The 'C' program for PICs has all the basic functions of a 'C' program, but there are also some specific instructions that are related to PICs, such as PORTAbits.RA0.

The main aspect of a 'C' program is that it runs inside a series of loops. There is a "main" loop from within which all the other loops, sometimes called functions, but I prefer to call them subroutines, are called from. The main loop must be there in the program as it is the "main" loop that the micro must go to at the very beginning of the program to get the first instruction of the program. The micro then carries out instructions in a sequential manner one after the other until it gets to the last instruction in the main loop. Unless this instruction forces the micro to go somewhere else, the micro will then go back to the first instruction in the loop then carry out all the instructions again in the same manner.

# The Comments and PIC Configuration

The first program we will look at is a very common task, that of waiting for a switch to be pressed, or turned on, and then lighting a LED connected to an output. However, before we can start our program, we should make sure

23

this program is our own. This is done by inserting some comments into the editing window. C programs use two main types of comments: single-line comments, which usually explain what the current instruction is doing, and multiple lines or a paragraph of comments, which give a more in-depth explanation.

The single comments are anything written on the current line following two forward slashes such as //.

Multiple-line comments are anything written between the following symbols /* */ as shown here, for example, /* Your Comments go Here*/

Having created your new 'C' file, the first thing you should do is insert some comments to tell everyone that this is your program and when you wrote it.

However, as this is a common starting point for programmers, the intelli-sense has put some comments in already. You may or may not wish to change them. However, to try and keep everything you see in your screens the same as they are in my screenshots, I suggest you delete everything that is currently in the text editing window so that you have an empty text window in the editor. You should now type in the following comments and commands so that your screen will be exactly the same as mine and my references will match up to your screens.

```
/* A basic program to turn on and off a led.

Written by Mr. H. H. Ward dated 28/07/2019 for the
18f4525 PIC

No modifications to date*/

#include <xc.h>

void main (void) {
    return;
}
```

Obviously, you should use your own name and the current date. Note also that as you write the text into the text editor, the intelli-sense will give the text the appropriate colors as there are different colors for different types of keywords.

These should be put into the top of your program file in the main editor window. This should take up the first nine lines, and the cursor should now be flashing at line ten ready for the next input.

Note that you can use these comments to keep track of any modifications that are being made and when they were made.

The next thing you need to do is tell the PIC how we intend to use some of its main variable attributes. This is because all PICs are very versatile in that among other things, they can be run from a wide variety of oscillators. Note that all instructions in the program and all other actions are synchronized to a clock signal. This clock signal can get its source from a wide variety of different oscillators from the simple low-frequency RC, resistor–capacitor, oscillator to the precise high-frequency crystal oscillator. These oscillator sources can be either external or internal to the PIC. The programmer needs to tell the PIC which oscillator they want to use. There are also other parameters the programmer needs to choose from. All this is achieved by writing the correct data to the config registers in the PIC as it is the data in these registers that configure how we are going to use the PIC. This can be achieved using a special window in the MPLABX IDE. To open this window, click on the word "Window" on the main menu bar then select "Target Memory Views" from the drop-down menu, then select Configuration Bits from the slide-out menu that appears. Once this is done, your main window will change to that as shown in Figure 2-13.

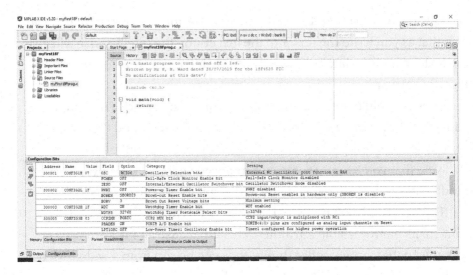

***Figure 2-13.*** *The Main Editing Window with the Configuration Bits Window Open*

You may have to drag the window up to make it larger as shown. I must apologize at this point, as I will not be showing you how to move the windows about inside the MPLABX IDE.

This configuration window allows you, as the programmer, to select some very important options for the PIC, the most important being the primary oscillator type and source used and if we want the watchdog timer or not.

There are three main options we need to change at this point. You should change the OSC to 'INTIO67' this is done by selecting the small arrow alongside the box next to the OSC option. The default setting is usually RCI06, the resistor-capacitor oscillator with bit 6 on PORTA left as a normal input–output bit. We need to change this. When you click on the small arrow, a small window will open. If you move the selection up to the next one, it will be the one we want, INTIO67, which means use the internal oscillator block as the primary source and leave bits 6 and 7 on PORTA as normal input–output bits. Therefore, click the mouse on the term INTIO67 to change the oscillator to this option.

The other changes are simpler as we need to set the WDT to 'OFF'. It important to turn the WDT, watchdog timer, off as if nothing happens for a predefined period of time in a program then the WDT will stop the program. We don't want this to happen, so we must turn the WDT off. This is done by clicking the mouse on the small arrow next to the WDT and clicking the mouse on the off option.

The final option I usually change is the LVP, "Low-Voltage Programming" option. I usually turn this off. This is turned off in the same way as the WDT was turned off

Once you have changed these setting, we can generate the source code, and then paste this code into our program. Click on "Generate Source Code to Output" tab shown at the bottom of the IDE. The source code should appear in the output window on the screen. Use the mouse to select all this code, then copy it all, and paste it into the "myFirst18FProg.c" c file you have in the open window. You should paste all the different configuration words and the comments as well into your 'C' file, but you don't need to copy the "#include <xc.h> " line as the intelli-sense has already put this in. We will learn the importance of that "#include <xc.h> " line soon. I have pasted these source instructions into my open file window starting at line 5 and ending at line 62. This moves the "#include <xc.h> " down to line 63. Yours may differ due to what comments you have put in.

Your screen should look like this as shown in Figure 2-14.

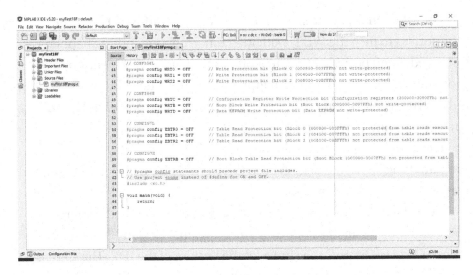

**Figure 2-14.** *The Configuration Listing*

The #include <xc.h> is important as we need to tell the compiler we want to use some labels to represent any addresses we will be using. The most important addresses we will use are the addresses of the SFRs, Special Function Registers. It is with these SFRs that the programmer can control every aspect of the PIC with the '1's and '0's that they write to these control registers.

The compiler really wants to use the address of the registers. However, we humans may want to use labels to give the register's names instead of using the actual address number.

An example of using a label is PORTA. This is a SFR at the address 0XF80 in this PIC. The compiler only needs the hexadecimal number "F80"; note that the "0X" stands for hexadecimal. However, to make the program easier for us humans to read, we would want to use the label PORTA. To enable this to happen, we have to tell the compiler that this label, and the others' labels, represent the correct address of the SFRs. There is a simple instruction that does this which is

EQU PORTA 0XF80.

This tells the compiler that the label PORTA actually means the number F80 in hexadecimal format.

To help us do this, and save a lot of work, someone has written the EQUs for all the labels for all the SFRs we could use. However, to use these equates, we need to tell the compiler to include them in our program. This is done by using the "#include <xc.h> " line in our program. Remember there is a "Linker" program in the IDE. This links together our own program and all the header files we tell the Linker program in "include"; but we MUST tell the linker program to include them.

This is inserted now into our program file. Later we might need to use other include files. We will explain the importance of this "#include <xc.h>" with an example later.

We are nearly ready to start writing our program. One very important thing to remember is that all 'C' and 'C++' programs use a collection of loops or functions or subroutines. This means we have to place all instructions inside these loops. The most important loop is the "main loop" as this is the first loop the micro goes to when the program is started. From this main loop, all the other loops, which I will call subroutines, which are used to carry out different aspects of the program, are called from.

## The TRISA and TRISB

The program is going to use two ports to communicate with the outside world. We will us PORTA as an input port, to which the two switches will be connected to, and PORTB as an output port, to which all the LEDS will be connected to. However, the PIC has no idea which way we want to use the PORTS. Each port can be either an input or output port. Indeed, we can mix them up much more as each individual bit in the port can be either input or output and with the 18F4525, each PORT has 8 bits. We, as the programmers, need to tell the PIC how we want to use the PORTS and their bits. This requires setting some of the I/O pins to input and some to output. Note that all PICs have at least two PORTS that can be used to allow the PIC to communicate to the outside world. The PORTS are identified as PORT A, B, C, and so on. Each PORT will have a number of individual bits that can be set to take data into the PIC, that is, be inputs, or to send data out of the PIC, that is, be outputs. An 8-bit PIC such as the 18F4525 has up to 8 bits on each PORT, whereas the 32-bit PICS have up to 32 bits per PORT. The PIC does not know which type you want the bits to be, either input or output.

You as the programmer must tell the PIC, by way of instructions in your program, which type you want the bits of each port to be. To enable you to do this, there are some SFRs, Special Function Registers, called TRIS which allow this to be done. There is a TRIS for each PORT, and each TRIS has the same number of bits as each PORT. The particular bit of each TRIS maps onto the same bit in the corresponding PORT as shown in Figure 2-15.

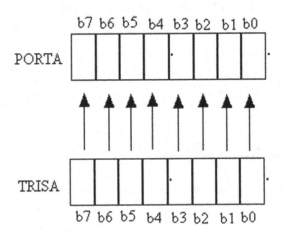

*Figure 2-15.* *The Mapping of the TRIS onto the PORT*

In this way the bits of the TRIS can control the corresponding bits of the PORT as to whether or not the bit in the PORT is an input or output. If the bit in the TRIS is a logic '1', then the bit in the PORT would be an input. If the bit in the TRIS is a logic '0', then the bit in the PORT would be an output.

# A TRIS Example

IF TRISA was set to 00001111, then bits 7, 6, 5, and 4 of PORTA would be outputs and bits 3, 2, 1, and 0 would be inputs. This assumes that the PORT has only 8 bits as with an 8-bit micro, and going from left to right, they are number b7, b6, b5, b4, b3, b2, b1, and b0.

# Exercise 2-1

What data would you have to write, to where, to set PORTC as Out, Out, In, Out, In, In, In, Out going from B7 down to B0 from left to right? Answers to all exercises are provided at the end of each chapter.

# Setting the PORTS

In our first program, we will make all the bits on PORTA inputs and all the bits in PORTB as output.

The following instructions, with their respective comments, will do what is required.

```
TRISA = 0xFF;      //Make all bits in TRISA a logic '1' which
                     makes all bits on  PORTA inputs
TRISB = 0x00;      //Make all bits in TRISB a logic '0' which
                     makes all bits on  PORTB outputs
```

Note that the 0x in front of the data means we are using hexadecimal numbers. This is because we only need to use 2 digits, as 1 hexadecimal digit represents 4 binary bits. It does not matter if we use lowercase letters or capital letters for these numbers.

Note also that we use the semicolon, ';' after the data OXFF. This indicates the end of the current instruction. Note also the use of single-line comments to explain what the instruction does; please be aware that in the text editor in MPLABX, these comments would be on one line.

The latter of the two instructions could have been written as follows:

TRISB = 0; This will make all the bits in TRISB a logic '0' which sets all the bits in PORTB to outputs. This is using the default radix, or number system, used in MPLABX, which is decimal. The instruction TRISB = 0; means the value stored in the TRISB would be zero which is 0b00000000 or 0X00.

One very important thing to note is that we are using capital letters in the word TRISA and TRISB; this is because this is how the labels have been defined in the include file we are using. Really the micro sees TRISA as the numeric value of 0XF92 which is where the SFR is in the PIC's memory.

NB: Note that '0X' in front of a number means that is a hexadecimal number, '0b' means it is a binary number, and no prefix means it is a decimal number. This is the same concept that MPLABX uses.

The include file has all the labels we will use for the SFRs, and they are all in capitals. For example, if we want to turn on all the LEDs, or any devices, connected to PORTB, we would have to write

PORTB = 0b11111111;

Note

portb = 0b11111111; would not work as the label for PORTB must be in capital letters.

Note that the '0b' stands for binary as we are stating the number in its binary format.

We could have written PORTB = 255, as this in decimal equivalent of 0b11111111 and decimal is the default radix for MPLABX .

# The ADC (Analogue to Digital Converter)

Most PICs, including ours, will have an ADC, Analogue-to-Digital Converter. This will be assigned to one of the PORTS, and this means that the inputs to the bits on that PORT could be analogue or digital. We as programmers must tell the PIC which we want the inputs to be: analogue or digital. In this case we want all the bits to be digital as they are simply high or low switches. For our 18f4525 PIC, it is PORTA that is assigned to the ADC and some of PORTB, as this PIC has 13 analogue channels. This means that the bits on PORTA, and some of PORTB, could be analogue or digital. The default setting is that they are all analogue. Note that an analogue input would be one connected to a transducer such as pressure or temperature transducer and would be a varying voltage used to represent the signal being monitored. We want all the bits on PORTA to be digital, that is, simply on and off signals, which would be logic '1' or logic '0' inputs. Therefore, we need to tell the PIC we want the bits on PORTA to be digital. Table 2-1 shows us that we can program the PORT to be one of many variations from all bits being analogue to all bits being digital.

***Table 2-1.*** *The Settings for Bits 3, 2, 1, and 0 of the ADCON0 8-Bit Register*

| Bit 7 | Bit 6 | Bit 5 | Bit 4 | Bit 3 | Bit 2 | Bit 1 | Bit 0 |
|---|---|---|---|---|---|---|---|
| Not Used | Not Used | VCFG1 | VCFG0 | PCFG3 | PCFG2 | PCFG1 | PCFG0 |
| Bit 7 | Not used read as 0 | | | | | | |
| Bit 6 | Not used read as 0 | | | | | | |
| Bit 5 | 1 negative reference from AN2 | | | | | | |
|  | 0 negative reference from VSS | | | | | | |
| Bit 4 | 1 negative reference from AN3 | | | | | | |
|  | 0 negative reference from VDD | | | | | | |

*(continued)*

*Table 2-1.* (*continued*)

| B3 | B2 | B1 | B0 | AN12 | AN11 | AN10 | AN9 | AN8 | AN7 | AN6 | AN5 | AN4 | AN3 | AN2 | AN1 | AN0 |
|----|----|----|----|------|------|------|-----|-----|-----|-----|-----|-----|-----|-----|-----|-----|
| 0 | 0 | 0 | 0 | A | A | A | A | A | A | A | A | A | A | A | A | A |
| 0 | 0 | 0 | 1 | A | A | A | A | A | A | A | A | A | A | A | A | A |
| 0 | 0 | 1 | 0 | A | A | A | A | A | A | A | A | A | A | A | A | A |
| 0 | 0 | 1 | 1 | D | A | A | A | A | A | A | A | A | A | A | A | A |
| 0 | 1 | 0 | 0 | D | D | A | A | A | A | A | A | A | A | A | A | A |
| 0 | 1 | 0 | 1 | D | D | D | A | A | A | A | A | A | A | A | A | A |
| 0 | 1 | 1 | 0 | D | D | D | D | A | A | A | A | A | A | A | A | A |
| 0 | 1 | 1 | 1 | D | D | D | D | D | A | A | A | A | A | A | A | A |
| 1 | 0 | 0 | 0 | D | D | D | D | D | D | A | A | A | A | A | A | A |
| 1 | 0 | 0 | 1 | D | D | D | D | D | D | D | A | A | A | A | A | A |
| 1 | 0 | 1 | 0 | D | D | D | D | D | D | D | D | A | A | A | A | A |
| 1 | 0 | 1 | 1 | D | D | D | D | D | D | D | D | D | A | A | A | A |
| 1 | 1 | 0 | 0 | D | D | D | D | D | D | D | D | D | D | A | A | A |
| 1 | 1 | 0 | 1 | D | D | D | D | D | D | D | D | D | D | D | A | A |
| 1 | 1 | 1 | 0 | D | D | D | D | D | D | D | D | D | D | D | D | A |
| 1 | 1 | 1 | 1 | D | D | D | D | D | D | D | D | D | D | D | D | D |

The table refers to the bits in the ADCON1 register which is an 8-bit register that controls certain aspects of the ADC.

The principle behind the ADC is that there is just one ADC circuit inside the PIC which can be switched to any one of the 13 inputs that can have an analogue input connected to it. This is a method termed "multiplexing" where the 1 ADC serves 13 possible analogue inputs. The ADC will then create a binary number that represents the actual voltage applied to the input. The ADC used in the PIC is a 10-bit ADC which gives the programmer a possible resolution of the following:

The resolution of the ADC is the smallest value that it can recognize. This can be calculated using the following expression.

$$\text{Resoluion} = \frac{Range}{2^n}$$
$$\therefore \text{Resoluion} = \frac{5}{2^{10}} = 4.883mV$$

That is if we used all 10 bits, and as this is an 8-bit micro, there is a problem with this, but we will look at that later.

The ADC is controlled by three registers; ADCON0, ADCON1, and ADCON2. The ADCON1 controls what voltage range is used and if the bit on the port is analogue or digital. The ADCON0 controls if the ADC is switched on and which bit or channel the ADC is connected to. The ADCON2 register controls the timing of the ADC; we will look at all these registers later.

We actually do not want to use the ADC, and we want all bits connected to PORTA to be digital; therefore, we should turn the ADC off and make all bits on PORTA and PORTB to be digital.

It is bit 0 of the ADCON0 register that turns the ADC on, that is, bit 0 = 1, or off, that is, bit 0 = 0. Therefore, make all bits of the ADCON0 register to logic 0. This will set $b_0$ to a logic '0' and so turn the ADC off.

It is bits 3, 2, 1, and 0 of ADCON1 register that determine if the bits on PORTA and PORTB are analogue or digital bits. This is shown in Table 2-1. If the bit in the ADCON1 register is a logic '0', then the input would be an analogue input. If the bit is a logic '1', then the input would be digital. This is a good example of how the actual bits are used to control the actions of the PIC.

As we need all the inputs to be digital, we need to make sure all these four bits, bits 3, 2, 1, and 0, in the ADCON1 register are set to logic '1'.

The following instructions will set the ADC up as we want.

```
ADCON0 = 0x00;  //This turns the ADC off
ADCON1 = 0x0F;  //This sets all the bits on PORTA and PORTB as
                  digital
```

Note that these instructions have comments which are separated from end of the instruction, signified by the semicolon ';', with the use of two forward slashes '//'. This signifies that everything written after these slashes on that current line are comments and are not compiled by the compiler software. The comments can be used to help describe what the instruction is doing.

The combination of the following four instructions will set the two ports as we want them:

```
TRISA = 0xFF;        //Make all bits in TRISA a logic '1' which
                       makes all bits on PORTA inputs
TRISB = 0x00;        //Make all bits in TRISB a logic '0' which
                       makes all bits on PORTB outputs
ADCON0 = 0x00;       //Makes all the bits in the ADCON0 logic '0'
                       This turns the ADC off
ADCON1 = 0x0F;       //This make bits 7,6,5 and 4 logic '0'
                       and bits 3,2,1and 0 logic '1'This sets
                       all the bits on PORTA and PORTB as digital
                       bits
```

# Setting Up the Oscillator

We have used the configuration words to tell the PIC we want to use the internal oscillator block as the primary oscillator source, that is, INTIO67. However, we have not told the PIC what oscillator we want to use. It is the bits in the OSCCON , OSCillator CONtrol register, that controls the internal oscillator block. There are eight possible oscillator frequencies we can use and it is bits b6, b5, and b4 which control the settings. We will set the oscillator to 8Mhz and make the frequency stable. To set the oscillator frequency to 8Mhz, we set the three bits, b6, b5, and b4, to a logic '1'. To make the frequency stable, we set bit 2 to a logic '1'.

We need to tell the PIC where it will get the signal for the system clock. There are three possible options as controlled by bits b1 and b0 of this register. This would give us three options, really four, but we only want three. However, as we have set the primary oscillator source in the configuration words to be the internal oscillator, then two options are the same. We can simply set these two bits to logic'0' as the primary source is the internal oscillator block.

> Bit 7 of the OSCCON register is the IDLEN bit which is used for sleep mode. We will not use this mode till much later; therefore, set this bit to a logic '0'.

> Bit 3 is actually a signal from the micro to the programmer so that this too can be set to a logic '0'.

This means that the eight bits in the OSCCON register can be set as follows:

```
OSCCON = 0b01110100;          //This sets the internal
                                oscillator to 8MHz and makes
                                it stable.
```

Tables 2-2 through 2-4 should help explain these settings

The device enters sleep when asked, and the system clock is from the primary oscillator. Sleep is a more advanced option, and it will be covered in my future books.

*Table 2-2.* *Use of OSCCON0 Register*

| Bit 7 | Bit 6 | Bit 5 | Bit 4 | Bit 3 | Bit 2 | Bit 1 | Bit 0 |
|-------|-------|-------|-------|-------|-------|-------|-------|
| IDLEN | IRCF2 | IRCF1 | IRCF0 | IOSTS | IOFS | SCS1 | SCS0 |
| LOGIC 1 Device enters sleep | See Table 2-3 | | | Logic 1 Time-out for osc startup Primary oscillator running | Logic 1 Internal oscillator is stable | See Table 2-4 | |
| Logic 0 device does not enter sleep | | | | Logic 0 No time out primary oscillator not running | Logic 0 internal oscillator not stable | | |

*Table 2-3.* *Bits 6, 5, and 4 of OSCON0 Register Setting the Oscillator Frequency*

| Bit 6 ICRF2 | Bit 5 ICRF1 | Bit 4 ICRF0 | Oscillator frequency |
|-------------|-------------|-------------|----------------------|
| 0 | 0 | 0 | 31kHz[1] |
| 0 | 0 | 1 | 125kHz |
| 0 | 1 | 0 | 250kHz |
| 0 | 1 | 1 | 500kHz |
| 1 | 0 | 0 | 1Mhz |
| 1 | 0 | 1 | 2MHz |
| 1 | 1 | 0 | 4MHz |
| 1 | 1 | 1 | 8MHz |

[1] *The 31kHz can be sourced from main oscillator divided by 256 or directly from internal RC oscillator*

*Table 2-4.* *The Usage of Bit 1 and Bit 0 of OSCCON0 Register to Select Source of Oscillator Frequency Signal*

| Bit 1 | Bit 0 | Oscillator source |
|-------|-------|-------------------|
| SCS1  | SCS0  |                   |
| 0 | 0 | Primary oscillator as defined in configuration words |
| 0 | 1 | Secondary timer block |
| 1 | 0 | Internal oscillator block |
| 1 | 1 | Internal oscillator block |

The process of deciding what data is written to the ADCON0, ADCON1, and the OSCCON shown earlier is an example of how you should determine what data is written to all the SRFs. You should decide what function you want the particular SRF to perform and write out on paper how you can either set it, write a logic '1', or clear it, write a logic '0', to each bit of the SRF to achieve what you need. Then write out the instruction in your program. It is a process that needs lots of practice.

## Exercise 2-2

Write down the 8-bit data that you think should be written to the OSCCON register to set the internal oscillator block to give a frequency of 500kHz, making the frequency stable and setting the internal oscillator block as the source for the system clock. The device does not enter sleep mode.

## Waiting for an Input

Now that we have set the PORTS up, we need to make the PIC wait until the switch connected to bit 0 of PORTA goes to a logic '1'. This will happen if the switch is set up so that when it is pressed, the logic level goes high, that is, to 5V or logic '1'.

There are a number of ways to do this, but it is basically testing the bit to see if it has gone high. The simplest way involves making the micro wait until the input goes high. Then when the input does go high, move on and do something.

You might think that you should keep on asking the question has the input gone high? The problem with this approach is that you must make the micro go back and ask the question again if the input has not gone high.

However, another way of looking at this test is to say that while the input is low or not high, do nothing. Indeed, this is the approach that we use in a 'C' program.

This can be done using a while command as shown here:

```
while (PORTAbits.RA0 == 0)
{
}
```

The concept of that while instruction is that while the test condition, written in BOLD only this one time to make it obvious what is meant by the test, expressed inside the normal brackets is true, carry out the instructions that are written between the curly brackets. In this case there are no instructions between the curly brackets, and so the micro does nothing.

We use the double = = sign to say it becomes equal to. This means the test is while PORTA bit 0 becomes equal to 0, the test is true, and so do what I say; in this case what is inside the curly brackets, which is nothing. In this way the instruction is saying that while the input on bit 0 of PORTA is at logic '0', do nothing.

Note that you can signify the bit of a PORT as shown earlier, that is, RA0 means bit 0 of PORTA.

Note also the specific syntax in specifying the actual bit of the PORT. This has to be correct or else the compiler will throw up an error.

An alternative way of writing the same instruction is

```
while (PORTAbits.RAO == 0) continue;      //Do nothing  while the
                                          logic at b0 of PORTA
                                          is at logic '0'.
```

This does exactly the same. Note also we use the ';' to donate the end of the instruction, and the only thing we are asking the program to do is continue which makes the micro go back to the start of the instruction.

Another alternative would be

while (!PORTAbits.RA0) continue;

In this case the Not operator '!' is used. The test is while the bit is NOT a logic '1' do what I tell you to do.

One final alternative to make the PIC wait until something happens, such as the logic at the input bit goes high, is

while (!PORTAbits.RA0) ;

This works in a similar fashion to the first example. There are no instructions between the closing normal bracket of the test and the end of the instruction, signified by the semi-colon ';'.

This then tells the micro to do nothing while the test inside the curly brackets is true. This is a very succinct way of getting the PIC to wait for something to happen. However, if you **unintentionally** put a semicolon after the closing bracket of the test statement, this could cause the program to get stuck here. Remember this when you are trying to debug a program that doesn't do what you want.

Using whatever format you like, the micro would stay in the while loop until the logic at bit 0 of PORTA went high. The micro would then move on to the next instruction of the program.

This would be to simply turn on the output at PORTB bit 0. This can be done using

```
PORTBbits.RB0 = 1;              //Turn on what is connected to b0
                                    of PORTB
```

# Waiting to Turn the LED Off

We can now make the PIC wait for a stop switch to be pressed so that the micro can then turn the output on bit 0 of PORTB off. This can be done as follows:

```
while (PORTAbits.RA1 == 0);     //Do nothing while the logic
                                    at bit 1 of PORTA is at
                                    logic '0'.
PORTBbits.RB0 = 0;              //Turn off what is connected
                                    to b0 of PORTB
```

Note that we must put all the instructions inside the main loop. The actual program instructions which start at 50 and end at line 58 of the program in Listing 2-1 should go inside the curly brackets of the editing window. To help you appreciate, this the screen should end up as shown in Figure 2-16.

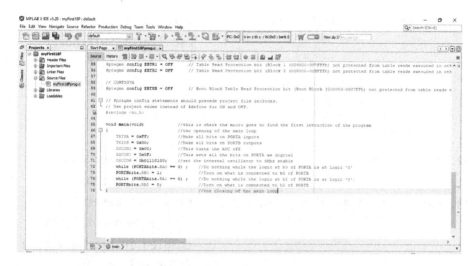

***Figure 2-16.*** *The Completed Editing Window*

Once we have written all the instructions for the first program, the editor window should look like the one shown here in Listing 2-1.

***Listing 2-1.*** The Completed LED Start Stop Program Instructions

1.  /*A basic program to turn on and off a led.
2.  Written by Mr H, H. Ward dated 28/07/2019 for the 18F4525 PIC
3.  No modifications at this date*/
4.
5.  // PIC18F4525 Configuration Bit Settings
6.  // C' source line config statements.
7.  // CONFIG1H
8.  #pragma config OSC = INTIO67     // Oscillator Selection
                                     bits (Internal
                                     oscillator block, port
                                     function on RA6 and RA7)
9.  #pragma config FCMEN = OFF       // Fail-Safe Clock Monitor
                                     Enable bit (Fail-Safe
                                     Clock Monitor disabled)

10. #pragma config IESO = OFF    // Internal/External Oscillator Switchover bit (Oscillator Switchover mode disabled)

11. // CONFIG2L
12. #pragma config PWRT = OFF    // Power-up Timer Enable bit (PWRT disabled)
13. #pragma config BOREN = SBORDIS    // Brown-out Reset Enable bits (Brown-out Reset enabled in hardware only (SBOREN is disabled))
14. #pragma config BORV = 3    // Brown Out Reset Voltage bits (Minimum setting)

15. // CONFIG2H
16. #pragma config WDT = OFF    // Watchdog Timer Enable bit (WDT disabled (control is placed on the SWDTEN bit))

17. #pragma config WDTPS = 32768    // Watchdog Timer Postscale Select bits (1:32768)

18. // CONFIG3H
19. #pragma config CCP2MX = PORTC    // CCP2 MUX bit (CCP2 input/output is multiplexed with RC1)

20. #pragma config PBADEN = ON    // PORTB A/D Enable B<4:0> pins are configured as analog input channels on Reset)

21. #pragma config LPT1OSC = OFF        // Low-Power Timer1 Oscillator Enable bit (Timer1 configured for higher power operation)

22. #pragma config MCLRE = ON           // MCLR Pin Enable bit (MCLR pin enabled; RE3 input pin disabled)

23. // CONFIG4L

24. #pragma config STVREN = ON          // Stack Full/Underflow Reset Enable bit (Stack full/underflow will cause Reset)

25.#pragma config LVP = ON              // Single-Supply ICSP Enable bit (Single-Supply ICSP enabled)

26. #pragma config XINST = OFF          // Extended Instruction Set Enable bit (Instruction set extension and Indexed Addressing mode disabled (Legacy mode))

27. // CONFIG5L

28. #pragma config CP0 = OFF            // Code Protection bit (Block 0 (000800-003FFFh) not code-protected)

29. #pragma config CP1 = OFF            // Code Protection bit (Block 1 (004000-007FFFh) not code-protected)

30. #pragma config CP2 = OFF          // Code Protection bit
                                      (Block 2 (008000-00BFFFh)
                                      not code- protected)

31. // CONFIG5H
32. #pragma config CPB = OFF          // Boot Block Code
                                      Protection bit (Boot
                                      block (000000-0007FFh)
                                      not code- protected)

33. #pragma config CPD = OFF          // Data EEPROM Code
                                      Protection bit (Data
                                      EEPROM not code-
                                      protected)

34. // CONFIG6L
35. #pragma config WRT0 = OFF         // Write Protection bit
                                      (Block 0 (000800-
                                      003FFFh) not write-
                                      protected)

36. #pragma config WRT1 = OFF         // Write Protection bit
                                      (Block 1 (004000-
                                      007FFFh) not write-
                                      protected)

37. #pragma config WRT2 = OFF         // Write Protection bit
                                      (Block 2 (008000-00BFFFh)
                                      not write- protected)

38. // CONFIG6H
39. #pragma config WRTC = OFF         // Configuration Register
                                      Write Protection bit
                                      (Configuration registers
                                      (300000-3000FFh) not
                                      write- protected)

40. #pragma config WRTB = OFF        // Boot Block Write
                                     Protection bit (Boot
                                     Block (000000-0007FFh)
                                     not write- protected)
41. #pragma config WRTD = OFF        // Data EEPROM Write
                                     Protection bit (Data
                                     EEPROM not write-
                                     protected)

42. // CONFIG7L
43. #pragma config EBTR0 = OFF       // Table Read Protection
                                     bit (Block 0 (000800-
                                     003FFFh) not protected
                                     from table reads executed
                                     in other blocks)
44. #pragma config EBTR1 = OFF       // Table Read Protection
                                     bit (Block 1 (004000-
                                     007FFFh) not protected
                                     from table reads executed
                                     in other blocks)
45. #pragma config EBTR2 = OFF       // Table Read Protection bit
                                     (Block 2 (008000-00BFFFh)
                                     not protected from table
                                     reads executed in other
                                     blocks)

46. // CONFIG7H
47. #pragma config EBTRB = OFF       // Boot Block Table Read
                                     Protection bit (Boot
                                     Block (000000-0007FFh)
                                     not protected from table
                                     reads executed in other
                                     blocks)

48. #include <xc.h>                    //the directive to include the
                                        header file xc.h

49. void main()                        //this is where the micro goes to
                                        find the first instruction of the
                                        program

50. {                                   //the opening of the main loop

51. TRISA = 0xFF;                       //Make all bits on PORTA inputs

52. TRISB = 0x00;                       //Make all bits on PORTB outputs

53. ADCON0 = 0x00;                      //This turns the ADC off

54. ADCON1 = 0x0F;                      //This sets all the bits on PORTA
                                        and PORTB as digital

55. OSCCON = 0b01110100;                //set the internal oscillator to
                                        8Mhz stable

56. while (PORTAbits.RA0 == 0) continue;    //Do nothing while
                                            the logic at b0
                                            of PORTA is at
                                            logic '0' When it
                                            goes to a logic
                                            '1' move to next
                                            instruction.

57. PORTBbits.RB0 = 1;                      //Turn on what is
                                            connected to b0
                                            of PORTB

58. while (PORTAbits.RA1 == 0) continue ;   //Do nothing while
                                            the logic at b1
                                            of PORTA is at
                                            logic '0'. When
                                            it goes to a
                                            logic '1' move to
                                            next instruction.

```
59. PORTBbits.RB0 = 0 ;                    //Turn off what is
                                             connected to b0
                                             of PORTB
60. }                        //the closing of the main loop
```

Note that this is the only time I will show all the instructions including the configuration words and the include directive lines 1 to 49. However, every program will need these configuration words and that #include <xc.h> line, they must be in all the programs. Later, I will show you how to create a header file for these instructions.

There is one rather subtle problem in this program. The problem is when the micro gets to the last instruction in the loop, it will go back to the first instruction in that loop and start all over again. This means that it will set up the ports, the ADC, and the oscillator again even though we have already set them as required, and there is no need to this. To prevent this from happening again, we can insert an unconditional loop that keeps the micro using all the other instructions forever but only runs the first five setup instructions once.

This is done by using another while instruction. The format is shown in Listing 2-2.

**Listing 2-2.** The While (1) Loop Inserted

```
61.   void main()            //this is where the micro goes to
62.   find the first instruction of the program
63.   {                      //the opening of the main loop
64.   TRISA = 0xFF;          //Make all bits on PORTA inputs
65.   TRISB = 0x00;          //Make all bits on PORTB outputs
66.   ADCON0 = 0x00;         //This turns the ADC off
67.   ADCON1 = 0x0F;         //This sets all the bits on PORTA
68.   as digital
69.   OSCCON = 0b01110100;   //set the internal oscillator to
                               8Mhz stable
```

70.    while (1)                  //While the result of the test
                                  is true do what is inside the
                                  curly brackets. Note the result
                                  of the test will be a logic'1'
                                  if it were true and a logic'0'
                                  if it were untrue. The test is
                                  specified inside the normal
                                  brackets. This test is simply a
                                  logic'1' which will always be
                                  true  as it is always a logic '1'
                                  This means the micro will always
                                  carry out the instruction inside
                                  the curly brackets. That is why
                                  it is called the forever loop. It
                                  will always be true and the micro
                                  will carryout the instructions
                                  written between the two curly
                                  brackets forever.

71.    {                         //the opening curly bracket of the
                                  for ever loop

72.    while (PORTAbits.RA0 == 0) ;   //Do nothing while the
                                      logic at b0 of PORTA is
                                      at logic '0'

73.    PORTBbits.RB0 = 1;        //Turn on what is connected to
                                 b0 of PORTB

74.    while (PORTAbits.RA1 == 0) ;        //Do nothing while the

75.    logic at b1 of PORTA is at logic '0'.

76.    PORTBbits.RB0 = 0;        //Turn on what is connected to
                                 b0 of PORTB

77.    }                         //the closing of the for ever
                                 loop

78.    }                         //the closing of the main loop

The while (1) loop, between lines 70 and 80, will carry out the instructions given inside the curly brackets if there are more than one instructions as long as the test is true. For the test to be true, the logic result of the test must be a logic '1'. It is fairly obvious that the result of the test (1) is always going to be a logic '1', and so the micro must always carry out the instructions written inside the curly brackets. That is, this is a forever loop, or, more correctly, an unconditional loop.

This means that the micro will carry out the first five instructions that are outside this while (1) loop, but from then on the micro will be stuck inside the while (1) loop, and so it will never carry out the first five instructions again. Great as this is exactly what we want.

Note also that in lines 72 and 74, the word continue has been removed as it is not needed. The instruction still does nothing, while the test is true as there are no instructions between the closing bracket, of the test statement, and the semicolon. Note that the semicolon denotes the end of the current instruction.

## Exercise 2-3

What would happen if we had put a semicolon after the test bracket on line 70 of the listing? For example, we wrote the following:

while (1); at line 70.

You should be aware that the configuration commands and the #include <xc.h> have been omitted from the program listing shown above, but they are there as they must be included in your project. Your program will always need some configuration commands and include commands.

# Comments

It is important to use comments in a good program, as they can explain what some of the instructions are doing and also give ownership to a program; after all it is your work so own it.

We can identify comments using the two forward slashes as //. Everything on that line after the two // is simply a comment, and the compiler program simply ignores them. In this way, we can identify single-line comments.

We can also identify a collection of lines such as a paragraph of comments, as anything that inserted between the following symbols, /* */, will be treated as comments.

In every program you write, you should state your ownership of it and the date when you wrote it. It is also useful to give a brief description of what it is doing and what PIC it was written for.

The following is a suggestion of what you should insert at the top of your c file. Note that the software may have automatically written some of these in for you, so modify them as you desire.

/* A basic on off switch to turn on or off an LED.

Written for the 18f4525 PIC

Written by "Your name"

Dated "To days date" */

# Testing the Program

Obviously we will test most programs with the use of the prototype board or a suitable ECAD program, but in this instance, we will use the simulation debug tool to test the program.

To test the program, we need two switches; the 'on' switch connected to RA0 and the 'off' switch connected to RA1.

The MPLABX software allows us to define switches using the "Stimulus" option which we can find from the "Window" option on the main menu bar and the "Simulator" item from the drop-down menu as shown in Figure 2-17.

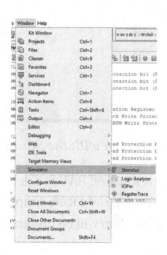

***Figure 2-17.*** *The Stimulus Window Option*

When we select this option, the screen should look like that as shown in Figure 2-18.

***Figure 2-18.***  *The Editing Screen with the Stimulus Window Open*

We can add the two pins RA0 and RA1 and define what action takes place when the inputs are fired. To add RA0, simply click the mouse on the empty box under the word pin. You will be presented with what is shown in Figure 2-19.

***Figure 2-19.***  *Selecting the PIN RA0*

You can scroll the small window down to find the pin RA0. We must set the action to toggle.

We can now add another row using the second tool icon in the stimulus window as shown in Figure 2-20.

*Figure 2-20.* *The Add Row Button*

You should end up with what is shown in Figure 2-21.

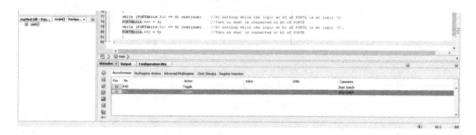

*Figure 2-21.* *The Completed Stimulus Window*

Note that there are two comments, one for each button that describes what the button does; you should type in a comment for the switch.

We can observe what happens by using the I/O pin option from the same simulator option from the drop-down menu from the Windows option in the main menu bar shown in Figure 2-17. Note that it might look a bit like 10Pin in the menu bar, but it is I O for Input/Output.

When using the I/O pin window, we can add which pins we want to look at. We should select RA0, RA1, and RB0. This is shown in Figure 2-22.

***Figure 2-22.*** *The Input Output PIN Selection Window*

It would be useful if we could see the program window, the stimulus window, and the I/O Pin window all at the same time. You can drag and move the stimulus window to try an arrange them as shown in Figure 2-23.

***Figure 2-23.*** *Showing All the Active Windows*

We are now ready to run our program and see what happens.

# Compiling and Running the Program

We have already selected the simulation as the programming tool, which was done in section "Creating the Project in MPLABX" as shown in

Figure 2-6. To run the program, we need to compile the program and run it. Compiling the program will test the syntax of the instructions and throw up errors, if there are any. It will also run the linker program that ensures any include files, such as the #include <xc.h>, which are compiled at the same time. The result will create a hex file that is used to program the actual PIC. However, in this case it will program MPLABX's simulator PIC.

We can, if you want, test the syntax of the program first by simply building the program. This is done by selecting the build option, which is a hammer symbol, from the main menu bar. This is shown in Figure 2-24.

***Figure 2-24.*** *The Build the Project Icon*

However, we could build and start the simulation in one operation. To carry out this process, you simply need to click the mouse on the Debug Main Project Icon in the menu bar as shown in Figure 2-25.

***Figure 2-25.*** *The Debug Main Project Icon*

During compilation a new output window should appear at the bottom of the MPLABX window. This shows the progress of the compilation. When it is complete, it will indicate where any errors are if they are any. If the compilation is successful, it should show that the user program is running.

We now need to simulate the switching action of the switches and then examine the reaction of the outputs. We can either add a watch table to examine the outputs or simply look at the I/O pins. Having successfully compiled the program, you should be able to test the operation of the program.

Click on the Debug Main Project icon as shown in Figure 2-25, and wait for the program to successfully compile. If there are errors, you should go back and check that you have typed everything exactly as shown above or in the complete program listing shown in the appendix. If an error does occur, the line would be shown in blue with an error message showing in the output window. If you click the mouse on that blue line, you should go directly to that line in the editing window where the error is. You must be very careful and make sure you have typed everything, apart from any comments, exactly as shown in the text, as shown in program Listing 2-2.

Assuming your program compiles correctly the output window should state that the program is running. You now need to fire the start, on, button and then the stop, off, button. Note that you are trying to simulate momentary switches that only close as long as you keep your finger on the button. To simulate this with the stimulus, you need to click the mouse on the fire button for that switch twice. The first click sends the logic high. The second click sends the logic back to zero. When you do this, you should see the I/O pins on RB0 and RA0 go green which means it has turned on. You now need to click the mouse on the RA0 pin again which will make the logic at that pin go to logic '0'. You should see the green light on the RA0 I/O pin go out but the green light on the RB0 stay green.

In this way you have simulated pressing the momentary start switch.

If you now carry out the same process on the stop switch, you should see the green light on RB0 go out and the green light on RA1 come on and then go out.

In this way you have simulated the stop switch being momentarily pressed.

If you now repeat the whole process, you should see the green lamps on the I/O come on and off correctly. This means you have successfully created and written your first C PIC program. Well done.

# Testing the Program Practically

This program is probably one of the simplest programs you can write; I hope you have found it fairly simple. So really there is no need to build a practical circuit for this. It may be more exciting to build a practical circuit of a set of traffic lights which is a program we will write very soon.

However, I will use this program to introduce you to the process of using an ECAD package to test the program. The ECAD package I will use is PROTEUS with the 8-bit micro package added to it.

This text does not teach you how to use PROTEUS; that is a book of its own. However, it will show you how to download your program to the PIC in the software, and it will help explain how you can connect the switches to the PIC.

The PROTEUS schematics for this first program is shown here in Figure 2-26.

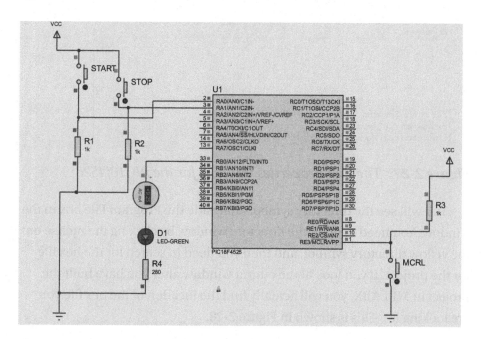

***Figure 2-26.*** *The Proteus Schematic for myFirst18fProg*

To download the program to the PIC in the schematic, you should click the mouse on the PIC to select it. Note that the simulation should not be running and the PIC will turn red when selected. Now click the right mouse button, on the PIC, and select edit properties from the drop-down menu that appears. You should now have the following window, shown in Figure 2-27, displayed.

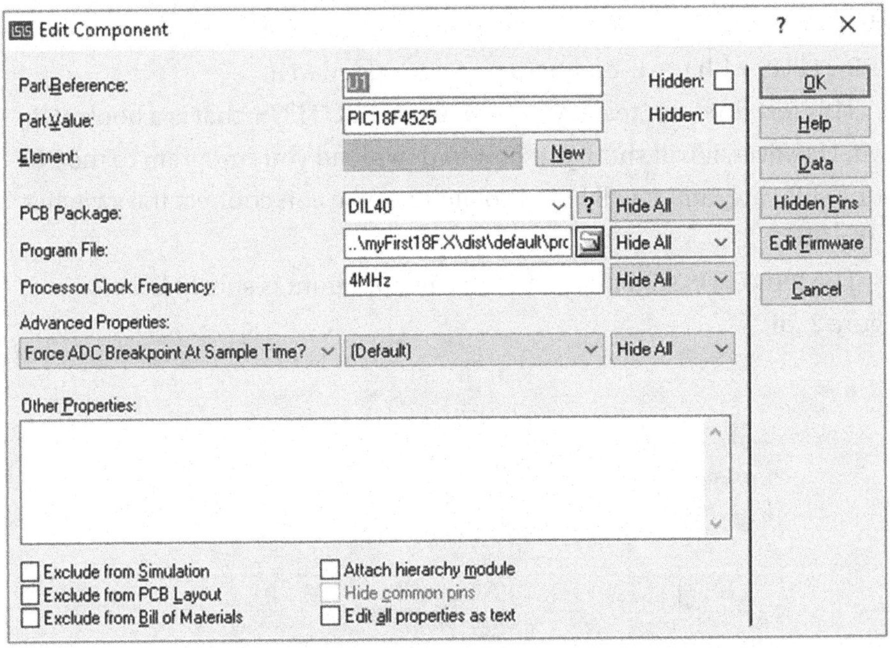

*Figure 2-27.* *The Edit Properties Window for the PIC18f4525*

You will see the directory symbol alongside the Program File box in the window. You need to open the directory window by clicking the mouse on the yellow directory symbol, and then you need to search for the hex file for the project. If you look at the output window after you have built the project in MPLABX, you will actually find the location of the hex file you are looking for. This is shown in Figure 2-28.

**Figure 2-28.** *The Path for the Hex File to Download to PROTEUS*

It should be the only hex file in that directory. You should click open to insert that location into the Program File Box in the properties window in PROTEUS. Once you have it in there, click the OK button, and you should return to the schematic window. You should now be able to run the simulation by clicking the play button. The program should work as expected.

If you have the correct software for PROTEUS, this should become a very useful method of running your program without buying a lot of equipment. You can simulate almost any PIC program you write using this software.

One very important aspect we can learn from the schematic is the use of the resistors R1, R2, R3, and R4. R1 and R2 are related to the two inputs. The input to the PIC is digital which means it will be a logic '1', that is, 5V or a logic '0', that is, 0V. This means there must be a path to either of those two voltages for the input. One path will become active when the button is pressed, and the other must be active when the button is not pressed. Note that you should never leave a bit on the port your program is using unconnected. This is termed floating. If you do leave it floating, it will inevitably float to the wrong logic level and may disrupt your program. With the RA0 input, the input goes to 0V logic '0' if the button is not pressed. This must be true as no current flows out of the PIC as it is an input, and so no current flows through R1. This means that the voltage at the top of R1, that is, at the input RA0, is the same as the voltage at the bottom of the resistor, as no current flows through it. As the voltage at the bottom of R1 is ground, then the input voltage to RA0 is also ground or 0V.

When the start button is pressed, the top of R1 which is connected to the input at RA0 is connected directly to VCC which is +5V. This means the voltage at RA0 goes to +5V which is the logic '1.'

Note the resistor R1 is there to limit the current through the switch to 5mA, and so protect the actual switch itself. This arrangement is termed pull up as closing the switch pulls the voltage up to VCC when the switch is closed.

When the start button is pressed, the top of R1 which is connected to the input at RA0 is connected directly to VCC which is +5V. This means the voltage at RA0 goes to +5V which is the logic '1.'

The same arrangement is used for RA1 and even the MCLR input. However, the switch at the MCLR input is termed pull down as it pulls the switch down to 0V when the switch is closed.

With the output, on RB0, the logic '1' condition puts 5V out to the top the green LED. To actually turn on, the LED drops around 2.2V across it but only needs around 10mA of forward current to glow. This means that as 2.8 volts is left to be dropped across the resistor R3; then its value is set to 280Ω to limit the current to 10mA.

NB: As a precaution against sparks or high-frequency noise affecting the supply to the PIC, you should connect a 100nF capacitor between the VCC and ground, placing the capacitor very close to the VCC pin of the PIC. This is not shown in the PROTEUS simulation, but it is there.

# Summary

I know there is a lot to take in, but becoming a real embedded programmer, who fully understands what they are doing, is a real challenge. There is a lot of text to read and maybe reread, but if you stick with it and complete all the tasks inside this book, I am sure you will find you are well equipped to enter this exciting, challenging, and rewarding career as an embedded programmer.

In this first task, you have studied the following:

- How to create a project in MPLABX.

- You have studied how to set up the ports correctly.

- How to set up the oscillator.

- You have studied how to use the datasheet to determine the settings for the control registers inside the PIC.

- You have studied how to use MPLABX's own simulator to test some aspects of your program.

So you have studied quite a lot, and that is why there is a lot to read and reread. Note that I say studied not learnt because to learn it, you will have to practice the procedure again and again. There will be different programs where you should create new projects, and this will help you learn that skill. I will not take you through the process again in the text of creating a project, but I will assume you have carried out that part again from scratch yourself, the whole process of creating the project and editing the program.

## Exercise Answers

Exercise 2-1: Write 0b00101110 or 0x2E to TRISC

Exercise 2-2: The 8-bit number for the OSCCON is 00110111 or 0X37

Exercise 2-3: The program would stop at this line as the semicolon denotes the end of the instruction and we are basically, say, forever simply do nothing.

# CHAPTER 3

# Updating the Program

In this chapter, you will be creating two new programs. The first one will look at creating a simple delay to delay when the lamps turn on and off. The second will extend the delay by creating a variable delay subroutine. After reading this chapter, you should be able to save a new updated version of a program while keeping the old one. You should be able to use the IF instruction and understand the difference between the IF and the while instruction. You will be able to use the GOTO instruction and the "for do" loop instruction.

You will be able to write a program that uses a subroutine with local and global variables.

## If This Then Do That

This first program can be used to show us how the programmer can use the IF This Then Do That Else Do something else concept in 'C.' The two switches on PORTA.RA0, the start switch, RA1, and the stop switch, give the user two options. If the start switch is pressed, then turn the output on. If the stop switch is pressed, then turn the output off. It really gives a third option which is that if no switches are pressed, then go back and check again. While this may be obvious, there is a slight difference in the approach to this program and the first program that used the

© Hubert Henry Ward 2020
H. H. Ward, *C Programming for the PIC Microcontroller*,
https://doi.org/10.1007/978-1-4842-5525-4_3

while statements. The program can be implemented using the IF Else statements. The text for the instructions follows:

```
Start:              if (PORTAbits.RA0 == 1) goto On;
                    if (PORTAbits.RA1 == 1) goto Off;
                    else goto Start;
On:                 PORTBbits.RB0 = 1;
                    goto Start;
Off:                PORTBbits.RB0 = 0;
```

Note that there is really no need to include the 'then' and the 'else' statements as the 'C' compiler knows that an 'If' keyword uses the 'then' and 'else' statements. However, there may be times when you should include the 'else' statement, but they are few and far between.

# Saving the Old Program

The preceding text has been put into the program listing overwriting the existing part of the program that is in the forever loop. Listing 3-1 is what your second program should look like.

However, it is good practice when changing anything to keep both the old program and the modified program. This is because sometimes your changes don't work and you want to go back to the old program before you made the changes. Therefore, you should click the "Save As" option and save the file as **mySecond18fprog.c**. which is a different name for the program.

*Listing 3-1.* The Modified Program

```
1.  void main()          //this is where the micro goes to
                          find the first instruction of
                          the program

2.  {                    //the opening of the main loop
3.  TRISA = 0xFF;         //Make all bits on PORTA inputs
4.  TRISB = 0x00;         //Make all bits on PORTB outputs
```

```
5.  ADCON0 = 0x00;              //This turns the ADC off
6.  ADCON1 = 0x0F;              //This sets all the bits on PORTA
                                  as digital
7.  OSCCON = 0b01110100;        //set the internal oscillator to
                                  8Mhz stable
8.  while (1)                   //the for ever loop
9.  {                           //the opening of the for ever loop
10.     Start: if (PORTAbits.RA0 == 1) goto On;
                                //if RA0 goes to logic '1' goto
                                  the label On
11.     if (PORTAbits.RA1 == 1) goto Off;
                                //if RA1 goes to logic '1' goto
                                  the label Off
12.     else goto Start;
                                //if none of the switches are
                                  pressed goto to the label Start
13.     On:   PORTBbits.RB0 = 1;
                                //turn the led on
14.     goto Start;             // goto to the label Start
15.     Off: PORTBbits.RB0 = 0;  //turn the led off
16.     }                       //the closing of the for ever loop
17.     }                       //the closing of the main loop
```

You should be aware that the configuration commands and the #include <xc.h> have been omitted from the program listing shown earlier, but they are there as **they must be included in your project. Your program will always need some configuration commands and include commands**.

You will now have two 'C' program files in the source files folder for this project. Don't worry if you didn't use the Save As option. It does not really matter if you have just overwritten the first program and just saved it over the old one. However, if you have used the Save As option, you will have two source files, but the one you have just saved is not showing in your project tree under source files. You will need to swap the old source file in the project tree window to the new file you have just created, **before** you compile the program again. To do this right, click the mouse on the source file selection from within the project tree. The follow menu bar will fly out as shown in Figure 3-1.

***Figure 3-1.*** *The Source Fly-Out Menu*

Using that fly-out menu, select "Add Existing Item." This will open the directory for this project, and you will need to open the 'C' file **mySecond18fProg** that you have just created. You will now have two 'C' files in the source directory in the project tree. You now need to remove the myFirst18fProg.c. To do this, simply right click the mouse on that file, and select the remove from project option from the pop-up menu. Note that the file will still be in your project folder on the hard drive; it just will not be used in the program. You now have just the **mySecond18fProg.c** in the source directory. Like everything new, there is a lot to learn, but after a few attempts, this process will be quite easy to do, and believe me you will most likely be very glad you have done it.

You can now rebuild the project by clicking on the debug main project icon and test the program out with the stimulus and I/O window.

Check it out and confirm it works as expected.

## Labels and the Goto Instruction

The second program we have written, mySecond18fProg.c, uses the new keyword "goto". Note that the 'C' programming language uses keywords, and the MPLABX IDE software identifies these keywords by writing them in blue. We will look at keywords more as we use them in later chapters of the book.

This new keyword, goto, forces the microprocessor to jump out of its normal sequential operation of the instructions and go to another part of the program. However, for the microprocessor to know where to go to, the complete instruction needs a label that corresponds to the section of program it should go to. In this way, labels and the goto keyword are linked together.

The label associated to the goto is written with the colon placed after it; look at the two labels, On: and Off:, in the program Listing 3-1 at lines 13 and 15. They both have the colon written after them. Therefore, the label tells the microprocessor where to go to with the goto keyword. Note that the full instruction should use the goto with the label as shown in lines 10, 11, 12, and 14 in Listing 3-1.

The goto keyword is a powerful tool, but care must be taken when using it.

## Exercise 3-1

Explain why the instruction goto Start; is required on line 14, between the ON and the OFF instructions in Listing 3-1. All exercise answers are provided at the end of the chapter.

## While vs. If Then

The main difference is that with the while instruction, the microprocessor will always carry out the associated instructions for as long as the test is true. Whereas with the if then else instruction, the microprocessor will examine the if then else condition and either carry out the instruction written after the if() if the test is true or simply move on to the next instruction if the test is not true; it does not keep the micro trapped waiting for the test to become untrue. It is a subtle difference, but it is an important one.

# Slowing the Micro Down

One of the main problems with writing code for microcontrollers is that they carry out instructions very fast. With an 8Mhz oscillator, the PIC can carry out 2 million instructions in 1 second, as the actual clock the micro uses runs at is a quarter of the oscillator. This is far too fast for us humans. This really means we need to create a delay. This is not as simple as writing delay (1000) to create a 1-second delay. You really need to appreciate how the micro creates a delay.

The concept of how we create a delay is quite simple. If you remember playing hide and seek, you should appreciate that the seeker delays their start of looking for those that hide by counting up to a number. Well it is the same with the micro. All micros have special timer registers that simply increment their value after each clock cycle. In this way they simply count clock cycles, and so they can be used to create delays. There are only two things that control the length of the delay, and they are

1. The number the timer has to count up to

2. The rate at which it counts

The 18F4525 has four timer registers that are used in this way. Timer0, timer1, timer2, and timer3. Each timer has a register that holds the current value of the timer and is incremented at the specified frequency, based on the micro's clock, for that timer. Each timer has a control register that is used to specify how the timer operates. Timer0 is the main timer for creating delays, whereas the other three timers have other uses, but they could also be used for delays if required.

# T0CON Register

This is the control register for timer0 and it sets out how the timer is used. To appreciate how to set up the timer, we need to appreciate the following:

- Firstly, the clock, which produces the cycles that the timer counts, runs initially at a quarter of the oscillator.

- Timer0 can be set to be an 8-bit register which means it can only count up to 256 clock cycles, 0 to 255. When it tries to count the next clock cycle, after reaching 255, it goes back to 0; this is called "rolling over." When timer0 first rolls over, a rollover bit will be set, and this can be used by the programmer if they wished to.

- Timer0 can be set to operate as a 16-bit timer which means it can count up to 65536, that is, $2^{16}$.

- We can also apply pre-scalars to the timer which will actually slow the rate at which the timer counts by dividing the clock frequency further.

To help explain the process further, we will go through an example of creating a 1-second delay using the internal 8 MHz oscillator.

As the clock runs at a quarter of the crystal, the clock runs at 2MHz.

If we set the timer0 to be a 16-bit register, then the highest number it can count up to is 65536, that is, $2^{16}$. This means that as the clock is running at 2Mhz, the timer increments or counts one ever 500ns. Therefore, the length of the delay would be 65536 times 500ns which would be 32.768ms. Not long enough. We need to slow the timer down, which we can do by applying one of the pre-scalars. These are displayed in the datasheet along with the use of all the bits in the T0CON register as shown in Table 3-1.

*Table 3-1.* *T0CON Register (See Data Sheet)*

| Bit 7 | Bit 6 | Bit 5 | Bit 4 | Bit 3 | Bit 2 | Bit 1 | Bit 0 |
|-------|-------|-------|-------|-------|-------|-------|-------|
| TMR00N | T08BIT | T0CS | T0SE | PSA | T0PS2 | T0PS1 | T0PS0 |

| | |
|---|---|
| BIT 7 | 1 Enables Timer0 |
| | 0 Disables Timer 0 |
| BIT 6 | 1 Sets Timer 0 as an 8-bit register |
| | 0 Sets Timer 0 as a 16-bit register, that is, two 8-bit |
| | registers together |
| BIT 5 | 1 Transition on TOCK1 pin |
| | 0 Transition on internal clock cycle (CLK0) |
| BIT 4 | 1 means increment on negative edge |
| | 0 means increment on positive edge |
| BIT 3 | 1 Timer0 is not divided further by selected divide rate. |
| | 0 Timer0 is divided further by selected divide rate |

| BIT 2 - BIT0 | BIT 2 | BIT 1 | BIT 0 | **Selected Divide Down Rate** |
|---|---|---|---|---|
| | 0 | 0 | 0 | Divide Clock Down by 2 |
| | 0 | 0 | 1 | Divide Clock Down by 4 |
| | 0 | 1 | 0 | Divide Clock Down by 8 |
| | 0 | 1 | 1 | Divide Clock Down by 16 |
| | 1 | 0 | 0 | Divide Clock Down by 32 |
| | 1 | 0 | 1 | Divide Clock Down by 64 |
| | 1 | 1 | 0 | Divide Clock Down by 128 |
| | 1 | 1 | 1 | Divide Clock Down by 256 |

This is an 8-bit register and

Bit 7 is used to either enable the timer or switch it off.

Bit 6 controls whether the timer0 is an 8-bit or a 16-bit register; note that to create a 16-bit register, the PIC simply connects two 8-bit registers together.

Bit 5 controls which clock it counts.

Bit 4 controls whether it counts on the positive edge or negative edge of the clock cycle.

Bit 3 controls whether or not the pre-scalar is applied or not. To divide the clock down, we need to apply the pre-scalar.

Bits 2, 1, and 0 are used to set the required divide rate. The 3 bits giving us 8 possible divide rates, that is, $2^3 = 8$.

To successfully create our 1-second delay, we will select the maximum divide rate which is divide by 256. This means that timer0 now counts at a rate of 7821.5 Hz, 2MHz divided by 256. This means that to create a 1-second delay, timer0 needs to count up to 7821.

I prefer to use the timer frequency to determine how long one tick takes. One tick is simply the periodic time of the timer frequency, normally symbolized by 'T'. From what we should know about frequency 'F' and periodic time 'T', we can determine the time using

$$F = \frac{1}{T}$$

$$\therefore T = \frac{1}{F} \therefore T = \frac{1}{7812.5} = 128\mu s$$

This means it takes 128µs to count up to one. Therefore, the time to count up to 7182 is 7812x128E⁻⁶ = 0.999936 second. Near enough especially when you take into account the time taken to carry out the instructions. If you needed to be extremely accurate, you would have to take into account the time it takes to carry out these instructions, but for our purpose, this simple approach is good enough.

Therefore, to create a 1-second delay, we need to write the correct 8-bit word to the T0CON register. This need only be done once so it can be done in the same part of the program as setting up the ports and oscillator. We would then write the instructions to make the timer start at 0, and then count up to 7812 before we do anything else. To illustrate this, we will simply modify the first program so that the LED will come on 1 second after pressing the start switch.

# Adding a One-Second Delay

We need to set up the timer0 by writing the required 8-bit data to the T0CON register. The correct data is

- Bit 7 = logic 1 to enable the timer

- Bit 6 = logic 0 to make the register a 16-bit register so it counts up to 65536

- Bit 5 = logic 0 as we are using the internal oscillator

- Bit 4 = logic 0 to set it up for negative edge triggering

- Bit 3 = logic 0 so that we can apply the pre-scalar and so divide the clock down

- Bit 2 = Logic 1

- Bit 1 = logic 1

- Bit 0 = logic 1 so that we apply the maximum divide rate of 256

This means that the data we need to write to the T0CON register is 0b10000111 in binary or 0X87 for hexadecimal.

The instruction to do this is simply

T0CON = 0x87

Now all that is left to do is after waiting for the start switch to be pressed, we set timer0 back to 0, and then do nothing until timer0 has counted up to 7812. The instructions to perform this task are

```
TMR0 = 0;
While (TMR0 <7812);
```

The while instruction is a simple one-line instruction which tells the microprocessor to do nothing, as no instruction is given between the closing bracket and the semicolon, while the value in TMR0, timer 0 register, is less than 7812.

# Exercise 3-2

As an exercise, determine what data must be written to the T0CON register to use the timer as an 8-bit register, and apply a divide by 32 rate. How long would each tick take, and what would the maximum delay be with this arrangement. The completed set of instructions with this delay written in is shown Listing 3-2.

*Listing 3-2.* One-Second Delay Included

```
1.  void main(void)
2.  {                       //This defines the start of the
                               main loop
3.  TRISA = 0xFF;           //Make all bits on PORTA inputs
4.  TRISB = 0x00;           //Make all bits on PORTB outputs
5.  ADCON0 = 0x00;          //This turns the ADC off
6.  ADCON1 = 0x0F;          //This sets all the bits on PORTA
                               as digital
7.  OSCCON = 0b01110100;    //set the internal oscillator to
                               8Mhz stable
```

```
8.  TOCON = OX87;            //set TMRO to on and 16bit with max
                               divide rate Freq = 7812.5Hz
                               one tick takes 128us.
9.  while (1)                //The forever loop
10.     {                    //This defines the start of the
                               forever loop
11.     while (PORTAbits.RAO == 0) ;    //Do nothing while
                                          the logic at bo
                                          of PORTA is at
                                          logic '0'
12.     TMRO =0;                         //make sure TMRO
                                          starts counting
                                          from 0
13.     while (TMRO < 7812);             //Do nothing until
                                          TMRO has counted
                                          up to 7812. This
                                          equates to a one
                                          second delay
14.     PORTBbits.RBO = 1;               //Turn on what is
                                          connected to bo
                                          of PORTB
        while (PORTAbits.RA1 == 0) ;     //Do nothing while
                                          the logic at b1 of
                                          PORTA is at logic
                                          '0'.
15.     PORTBbits.RBO = 0;               //Turn on what is
16.                                       connected to bo
                                          of PORTB
17.     }          //This defines the end of the forever loop
18.  }             //This defines the end of the main loop
```

You should be able modify your first program to include the delay and T0CON instruction. You should then be able to simulate the program and confirm that it works as expected.

# Delaying the Turn Off

In this modification, we are going to add a one-second delay so that the lamp turns off one second after the stop switch has been pressed. This could be done by simply adding the on- second delay instruction after the wait for the stop switch to be pressed. This is shown in Listing 3-3.

*Listing 3-3.* Adding the Second One-Second Delay

```
1.  void main(void)
2.  {                       //This defines the start of the main loop
3.  TRISA = 0xFF;                //Make all bits on PORTA inputs
4.  TRISB = 0x00;                //Make all bits on PORTB outputs
5.  ADCON0 = 0x00;              //This turns the ADC off
6.  ADCON1 = 0x0F;             //This sets all the bits on
                                PORTA as digital
7.  OSCCON = 0b01110100;     //set the internal oscillator to
                                8Mhz stable
8.  T0CON = 0X87;            //set TMR0 to on and 16 bit with
                                max divide rate Freq = 7812.5Hz
                                one tick takes 128us.
9.  while (1)               //The Forever Loop
10.       {                 //This defines the start of
                                the forever loop
11.       while (PORTAbits.RA0 == 0) ;    //Do nothing while
                                            the logic at b0
                                            of PORTA is at
                                            logic '0'
```

| 12. | TMR0 =0; | //make sure TMR0 starts counting from 0 |
|---|---|---|
| 13. | while (TMR0 < 7812); | //Do nothing until TMR0 has counted up to 7812. This equates to a one second delay |
| 14. | PORTBbits.RB0 = 1; | //Turn on what is connected to b0 of PORTB |
| 15. | while (PORTAbits.RA1 == 0) ; | //Do nothing while the logic at b1 of PORTA is at logic '0'. |
| 16. | TMR0 =0; | //make sure TMR0 starts counting from 0 |
| 17. | while (TMR0 < 7812); | //Do nothing until TMR0 has counted up to 7812. This equates to a one second delay |
| 18. | PORTBbits.RB0 = 0; | //Turn on what is connected to b0 of PORTB |
| 19. | } | //This defines the end of the forever loop |
| 20. | } | //This defines the end of the main loop |

This would work fine but it is not the most efficient way of doing this.

# Using Subroutines

Whenever you are going to use the same instructions in **EXACTLY** the same way more than once, then instead of writing them in multiple places in the code as we have done in program Listing 3-3, it is better to write these lines in the form of a subroutine, which is a small self-contained section of code that lives outside the main program. The main program has to "Call" the subroutine from within the main program every time the main program wants to use the subroutine. Note that in 'C' these subroutines are called "Functions" or "Methods," but I prefer to call them subroutines.

# Defining and Calling a Subroutine

We define the subroutine in the same way as we define the main loop.

```
void delay()            //give the subroutine a sensible
                          name such as delay
{                       //opening curly brackets of the
                          subroutine
    TMR0 = 0;           //ensure timer 0 starts counting
                          from zero
    while (TMR0 < 7182);//whilst the value in timer 0
                          register is less than 7812 do
                          nothing
}                       //closing brackets of the
                          subroutine
```

# The delay Subroutine

At this point it would be useful to appreciate that, when we call a subroutine, we can pass information up to a subroutine and also receive information back from a subroutine. 'C' uses keywords to tell the program that a subroutine is going to send information back to the main program from a subroutine. The word "void" is a keyword that means this subroutine is not going to send any information back to the main program. Other keywords could be "int" or "char" which means the subroutine will send an integer, or a char, back to the main program.

The method by which we can show that the subroutine is requiring information to be sent up to the subroutine is by including it inside the normal bracket written after the name for the subroutine. An example of this will be given later.

The keyword "void" at the beginning of this subroutine means that it will not be sending anything back to the main program.

The next thing to do is give the subroutine an appropriate name. In this case it is called delay.

There are now two normal brackets, the opening followed by the closing bracket. These are left empty as this subroutine is not expecting any information to be sent up to it.

As this subroutine has more than a single-line instruction, there are the opening and closing curly brackets. The actual instructions of the subroutine are placed inside these curly brackets.

# Calling the Subroutine from Within the Main Program

This is quite a simple process; all you have to do is write the name of the subroutine you want the program to call. This is shown here:

```
delay ();   //this will call the subroutine "delay"
```

The normal brackets are required even if you are not sending any information to the subroutine, and so they **must** be there. Note that the semicolon indicates the end of the instruction.

The complete code for the first program with the two delays is shown in Listing 3-4.

*Listing 3-4.* First Program with Two Delays Using the Subroutine

```
1.  void delay()              //the delay subroutine
2.  {                         //the opening bracket of the
                                 subroutine
3.  TMR0 = 0;                 //ensure timer 0 starts counting
                                 from zero
4.  while (TMR0 < 7182);      //do nothing while the value of
                                 timer 0 register is less than 7812
5.  }                         //the closing bracket of the
                                 subroutine
6.  void main(void)           //the main program loop
7.  {                         //the opening bracket of the main
                                 loop
8.  TRISA = 0xFF;             //Make all bits on PORTA inputs
9.  TRISB = 0x00;             //Make all bits on PORTB outputs
10.     ADCON0 = 0x00;        //This turns the ADC off
11.     ADCON1 = 0x0F;        //This sets all the bits
                                 on PORTA as digital
12.     OSCCON = 0b01110100;  //set the internal oscillator
                                 to 8Mhz stable
13.     T0CON = 0X87;         //set TMR0 to on and 16 bit with
                                 max divide rate Freq 7812.5Hz
                                 one tick takes 128us.
14.     while (1)             //the forever loop
```

```
15.      {                              //the opening bracket of the
                                            forever loop
16.      while (PORTAbits.RA0 == 0) ;   //Do nothing while the
                                            logic at b0 of PORTA
                                            is at logic '0'
17.      delay();                       //call the delay
                                            subroutine
18.      PORTBbits.RB0 = 1;             //Turn on what is
                                            connected to b0 of
                                            PORTB
19.      while (PORTAbits.RA1 == 0) ;   //Do nothing while the
                                            logic at b1 of PORTA
                                            is logic '0'
20.      delay();                       //call the delay
                                            subroutine
21.      PORTBbits.RB0 = 0;             //Turn off what is
                                            connected to b0 of
                                            PORTB
22.      }                        //the closing bracket of the
                                       forever loop
23.      }                        //the closing bracket of the main
                                       loop
```

# The Variable Delay and the For Do Loop

In this extension of the program, we are going to create a variable delay. Also, as the version of PROTEUS I have only models 8-bit micros, I will change the TMR0 to be an 8-bit register as my version of PROTEUS will not model 16-bit micros. This will also introduce a very powerful loop, the "For Do Loop."

First of all, we need to change TMR0 to an 8-bit register. This is done by setting bit 6 of the T0CON register to a logic '1'. If we leave everything else as we set earlier, then the 8-bit value we need to write to the T0CON register is 0b11000111 or 0XC7. The instruction for this is

```
T0CON = 0XC7;
```

Now that we are using an 8-bit register, it means that the maximum value the TMR0 can count up to is 255. This means that the maximum delay this will give is $256x128E^{-6} = 32.768$ms. The way we can increase this to make a one-second delay is to repeat this delay approximately 30 times. Doing this 30 times will produce a delay of 983.04ms, almost 1 second. If we consider the time that the micro takes to carry out the instructions, then this delay is close enough to one second.

To make the micro repeat this 32.768-ms delay 30 times, we will make use of the "for do loop." The instructions to do this are written below:

```
for (n = 0; n <30; n++)
    {
    TMR0 = 0;
    while (TMR0 < 255);
    }
```

There are actually three instructions written inside the normal brackets of the "for" keyword. They are

n = 0; This sets the value of the variable 'n' to 0.

n < 30; This asks the question is n less than 30, and as long as n is less than 30, do what is written inside the curly brackets. The two instructions inside the curly brackets make up the new 32.768ms delay.

The last instruction inside the normal brackets is n++. This will simply increment the value of n by one every time the micro carries out the instructions inside the curly brackets.

To help explain what happens, we can look at the steps that the micro carries out.

1.  n is loaded with a value of 0.

2.  The micro asks the question is n less than 30, which of course it is now.

3.  Then the 32.768ms delay is carried out.

4.  Then the value of n is increased by 1.

5.  Then the micro asks the question is n less than 30. Note that 'n' now equals 1.

6.  If it is, then 3, 4, and 5 are carried out again.

There will be a time when n is not less then 30, that is, when it actually equals 30. At this point the micro will break out of the "for do loop," and the subroutine is finished.

This will now produce a one-second delay or very close to a one-second delay.

This is good, but it is not a variable delay as it is always comparing n to 30. The modification to make this a variable delay is to change the subroutine as follows:

```
void delay(unsigned char m)
{
    for (n = 0; n <m; n++)
    {
    TMRO = 0;
    while (TMRO < 255);
    }
}
```

Note that there is the term 'unsigned char m' inside the normal bracket. Also, the question inside the "for do loop" is now is n less than m. This means that the subroutine is asking for an unsigned char, to be passed up to the subroutine. The subroutine then uses this value to load into the variable 'm.' In this way if m was 30, we would have a 1-second delay. If m was 60, we would have a 2-second delay. Therefore, the length of the delay is set by the value given to the variable 'm.' However, as this is an 8-bit register, the maximum value we can give to the variable 'm' is 255. This is why the variable is defined as an unsigned char as this uses all 8 bits. An unsigned int, or integer, would use up 16 bits. See the section on data types in the Appendix.

One question you should be asking is what are 'n' and 'm'? These are variables, and the following text should explain what they are.

# Local and Global Variables and Data Types

When we declare a variable, we are really reserving a space in memory where we can store a value. If the variable is to represent a real quantity like pump1 speed, then you should give it a meaningful name such as pump1Speed to the variable.

Each variable will have a specific data type, and there are a wide range of data types to choose from. The most common ones are "char" "unsigned char" "int", unsigned int and "float", and so on. There is a full description of the data types in the Appendix. However, it would be useful at this point to compare the three common data types.

## Type Char

This uses an 8-bit memory location to store a range of values. However, the most significant bit, the MSB, is not used to determine the number. The char uses what is termed "signed number representation." This is where the MSB, that is, bit 7, is reserved to show if the number being stored is a positive or a negative number. If the MSB is a logic '0', then the number is positive. If the MSB is a logic '1', then the number is a negative number. Therefore, the value of a type "char" can go from

`11111111` which is `-127`

to

`01111111` which is `+127`.

The MSB is not used to be part of the actual number or value; it is only used to show if the number is positive or negative.

## Type Unsigned char

The type "unsigned char" does not reserve the MSB to represent the 'sign' of the number as all numbers will be positive. This means that a type "unsigned char" can hold a value from

`00000000` = `0`

to

`11111111` = `255`

## Type int

The last type "int" is a 16-bit number, but like the "char," it reserves the MSB to represent if the number is positive or negative. Therefore, a type "int" can hold a value from

`1111111111111111` = `-32768` to `0111111111111111` = `+32768`

It is important to appreciate all the different data types and the difference between signed and unsigned number representation.

In our program, as my version of PROTEUS only uses 8-bit micros, I will restrict all my variables to 8-bit variables and use type "unsigned char" unless I need to store negative numbers.

That is why I have named the variable 'm' as an "unsigned char."

# Local Variables

If we leave the variable 'm' being declared as it is, inside the normal brackets of the subroutine, then it will be a local variable which means it is only valid for use inside that subroutine. If we try to use the variable inside any other subroutine or inside the main loop of the program, then the compiler will say it does not recognize the variable 'm'.

# Global Variables

The other variable 'n' will be declared as a global variable. This means that the variable 'n' can be used anywhere in the program, that is, inside the main loop and any subroutines that the program uses. The complete listing to show how to declare these variables is shown in Listing 3-5.

*Listing 3-5.*  Using the Variable Delay Subroutine

```
1.  //declare all global variables this is just one way of
        breaking up the program listing into different sections.
2.  unsigned char n;            //reserve an 8 bit memory
                                  location for the variable 'n'
                                  This is a global variable
3.  //define any subroutine this is just one way of
        breaking up the program listing into different sections.
```

4.  void delay(unsigned char m)        //this subroutine expects a number to be passed up to it in the call to assign to the variable 'm'this is a local variable

5.  {        //opening curly bracket of the subroutine

6.  for (n = 0; n < m ; n++)        //sets n to 0, asks is n less than m. if it is carryout the instruction between the curly brackets.

7.  {        //opening curly bracket of the for do loop

8.  TMR0 = 0;        //set timer 0 register to 0

9.  while (TMR0 < 255);        //do nothing while TMR0 is less than 255 note an 8 bit  register can only count up to 255

10.        }        //closing curly bracket of the subroutine

11.        }        //closing curly bracket of the for do loop

12.        void main(void)        //the start of the main loop

13.        {        //opening curly bracket of the main loop

14.        TRISA = 0xFF;        //Make all bits on PORTA inputs

| 15. | TRISB = 0x00; | //Make all bits on PORTB outputs |
| 16. | ADCON0 = 0x00; | //This turns the ADC off |
| 17. | ADCON1 = 0x0F; | //This sets all the bits on PORTA as digital |
| 18. | OSCCON = 0b01110100; | //set the internal oscillator to 8Mhz stable |
| 19. | T0CON = 0XC7; | //set TMR0 to on and 8bit with max divide rate Freq = 7812.5Hz one tick = 128us. |
| 20. | while (1) | //the start of the for ever loop |
| 21. | { | //opening curly bracket of the for ever loop |
| 22. | while (PORTAbits.RA0 == 0) ; | //Do nothing while the logic at b0 of PORTA is at logic '0' |
| 23. | delay(30); | //call the delay subroutine making m = 30 |
| 24. | PORTBbits.RB0 = 1; | //Turn on what is connected to b0 of  PORTB |
| 25. | while (PORTAbits.RA1 == 0) ; | //Do nothing while the logic at b1 of PORTA is at logic '0'. |
| 26. | delay(15); | //call the delay subroutine making m = 15 |

```
27.        PORTBbits.RB0 = 0;          //Turn off what is
                                        connected to b0
                                        of  PORTB
28.        }                           //closing bracket of
                                        forever loop
29.        }                           //closing bracket
30                                       of main loop
```

**NB:** Note that as with all our programs, the #include <xc.h> and all the configuration words must be written above the code.

You should change the text in mySecond18fProg.c to that shown in Listing 3-5 and see how the program works. Note that the program should wait one second before the LED turns on and just half a second before the LED turns off. Can you see why?

This is because the delay for turning the LED on sets m to 30 and the delay for turning the LED off sets m to 15.

# Exercise 3-3

To reinforce the concept of local variables as opposed to global variable, try writing the following just after the line for PORTBbits.RB0 = 0 as follows:

```
m = 10;
```

Now try and build the program. You should see an error occur which points to that line. This is because the compiler does not recognize the variable 'm' as it is not a global variable; it is only a local variable for use in the subroutine delay (unsigned char m).

What would happen and why if you wrote?

n = 10; instead of

m = 10;

# Summary

This chapter has taken us from simply turning a lamp on and off to appreciating the complexities of creating a variable delay. It has introduced to the concept of creating and using subroutines.

This has now got us to the point where we are ready to create a project and program that control a simple set of traffic lights. This will be covered in the next chapter.

# Exercise Answers

Exercise 3-1: If that goto was not there, then the micro would simply move to the Off instruction immediately after carrying out the On instruction. This means that the micro would turn on the LED connected to RB0, then immediately afterward, it would turn off the LED connected to RB0. This means you would not see the LED turn on. The goto instruction forces the micro to go back to the start after it has turned on the LED. You could comment this instruction out by placing the two forward slashes '//' before the word goto, and see what happens when it is commented out.

Exercise 3-2: TOCON = 0b11000100 one tick = 16 microseconds max delay = 256x16u = 4.096msec.

Exercise 3-3: With n = 10; the program compiles correctly as n is a global variable.

# CHAPTER 4

# Applying What We've Learned

In this chapter we are going to apply what we have learnt in a simple program. It is probably the most common program that all new embedded programmers start with. It will take you through a structured approach to design programs.

After reading this chapter, you will be able to program a simple model of a set of traffic lights. You will be able to call subroutines from within the main program loop.

## Controlling a Single Set of Traffic Lights

Hopefully it should not be too much of a problem to design a program that would control a set of three lights, Red, Amber, and Green, to mimic a single set of traffic lights.

The first thing we need is a sequence of events and they are

- The RED lamp should come on when the program starts.

- Then 5 seconds later, the AMBER lamp should come on as well.

© Hubert Henry Ward 2020
H. H. Ward, *C Programming for the PIC Microcontroller*,
https://doi.org/10.1007/978-1-4842-5525-4_4

- Then 2 seconds later, the RED and AMBER lamps should go out, and the GREEN lamp should come on.

- Then 5 seconds later, the GREEN lamp goes out, and the AMBER lamp comes back on by itself.

- Then two seconds later, the AMBER lamps goes out, the RED lamp comes on, and the whole sequence starts again.

# The Algorithm

This task will require the following I/0:

- Three outputs for the three lamps of the traffic lights.

- It will use one timer to create a variable delay.

- We can use the internal oscillator block with the 8MHz internal oscillator.

- There is no need for the WDT, watchdog timer, as the watchdog timer is something that an industrial production line would need, not the sort of programs we will be writing.

- The main process of the program will be to set up the PIC and the ports, oscillator, and timer 0.

The program will continually go through the following sequence:

1.  Light the RED lamp.

2.  Call a 5-second delay.

3.  Light the AMBER lamp.

4.  Call a 2-second delay.

5. Turn off the RED and AMBER lamp, and turn on the GREEN lamp.

6. Call a 5-second delay.

7. Turn off the GREEN lamp, and turn on the AMBER lamp.

8. Call a 2-second delay.

9. Then turn off the AMBER lamp, and repeat the sequence again.

The flowchart for the program is shown in Figure 4-1.

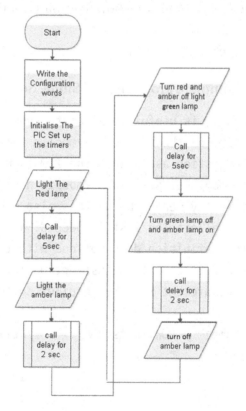

***Figure 4-1.*** *The Flowchart for the Single Traffic Light*

Flowcharts are an aid to designing programs as they split up the program into smaller sections that can be completed either with existing blocks of program or by different programmers.

They show how the program should flow from one part to the other. The connecting arrows should show the direction of flow from one block to the next. Each shape of the block has a special meaning.

When a flowchart extends across a page, then connecting symbols, which are circles with letters in them, can be used.

You should construct a flowchart for every program you design as if constructed fully, each block in the flowchart links into its own section of program listing and instructions.

However, to save space I will only show flowcharts for this program and the next one.

Listing 4-1 provides program listing.

***Listing 4-1.*** The Complete Program for a Single Set of Traffic Lights

```
1.    /*Definitions it is useful to allocate symbolic names to
      the actual bits on the I/O. The symbolic names should
      give some suggestion as to what the I/O is used for. Now
      wherever the compiler sees the symbolic name, it knows
      what I/O it really means. Doing this also makes it easier
      to change the allocation list if needed. Note that the
      line with the definition does not end with the semicolon.
      This is because it is not an instruction for the program,
      it is just a statement for the compiler software to be
      aware of.*/
2.    #define redLamp1    PORTBbits.RB0      //defines the
                                             symbolic name
                                             redLamp1 to mean
                                             bit 0 of PORTB
```

3.  #define amberLamp1  PORTBbits.RB1        //defines the
                                                symbolic name
                                                amberLamp1 to
                                                mean bit 1 of
                                                PORTB

4.  #define greenLamp1  PORTBbits.RB2        //defines the
                                                symbolic name
                                                greenLamp1 to
                                                mean bit 2 of
                                                PORTB

5.  //Global variables    //These are variables for anywhere in
                              the program

6.  unsigned char n;            //This reserves a memory
                                   location for the 8 bit
                                   variable 'n' using all 8 bits
                                   for the number

7.  //Subroutine

8.  void delay(unsigned char t)      //This is the start of
                                        a subroutine called
                                        delay. It expects a
                                        value to be passed
                                        up to the subroutine
                                        which it copies into
                                        the local variable
                                        't'.

9.  {                          //opening curly bracket of delay
                                  subroutine

10.     for (n = 0; n < t; n++)  //sets up a for do loop
                                    which controls how many
                                    times the micro carries
                                    out the instructions
                                    inside the curly brackets.

```
11.        {                  //opening curly bracket for the
                                  for do loop
12.        TMRO = 0;          //set TMRO to O. start value for
                                  count
13.    while (TMRO < 255); //while value of TMRO is less
                                  than 255 do nothing. Lines 12
                                  and 13 create a 32.77msec delay
14.        }                  //closing curly bracket for the
                                  for do loop
15.        }                  //closing curly bracket for the
                                  delay subroutine
16.    void main()  //start of the main loop
17.  {                  //opening curly bracket for main loop
18.        PORTA = 0;    //these few lines turn off all bits on
                            the PORTS
19.        PORTB = 0;
20.        PORTC = 0;
21.        PORTD = 0;
22.        PORTE = 0;
23.        TRISB = 0;    //This sets all bits on PORTB as outputs
24.        ADCONO = 0;    //turn ADC off
25.        ADCON1 = 0xOF;  //make all bits digital
26.        OSCCON = 0x74;  //set osc to 8Mhz with stable output
27.        TOCON = 0xC7;   //set TMRO to 8 bit reg with divide
                              by 256 rate so runs at 7812.5 Hz
                              one tick = 128uS
28.        while (1)       //start of the for ever loop so micro
                              only carries out lines 16 to 27
                              only once
29.  {                   //opening curly bracket of for ever
                              loop
30.        redLamp1 = 1;   //turns the redLamp1 on
```

```
31.        delay (153);      //calls the subroutine delay and pass
                               the value 153 up to the subroutine.
                               This creates a 5 second delay.
32.        amberLamp1 = 1;    //turns the amberLamp1 on
33.        delay (61);        //calls the subroutine delay
                               and pass the value 61 up to
                               the subroutine. This creates
                               a 2 second delay.
34.        redLamp1 = 0;      //turns the redLamp1 off
35.        amberLamp1 = 0;    //turns the amberLamp1 off
36.        greenLamp1 = 1;    //turns the greenLamp1 on
37.        delay (153);       //calls the subroutine delay
                               and pass the value 153 up to
                               the subroutine. This creates
                               a 5 second delay.
38.        greenLamp1 = 0;    //turns the greenLamp1 off
39.        amberLamp1 = 1;    //turns the amberLamp1 on
40.        delay (61);        //calls the subroutine delay
                               and pass the value 61 up to
                               the subroutine. This creates
                               a 2 second delay
41.        amberLamp1 = 0;    //turns the amberLamp1 off.
                               Micro now goes back up to
                               line 28 and repeats the loop.
42.        }                  //closing bracket of for ever
                               loop
43.        }                  //closing bracket of for main
                               loop
```

The PROTEUS simulation is shown in Figure 4-2.

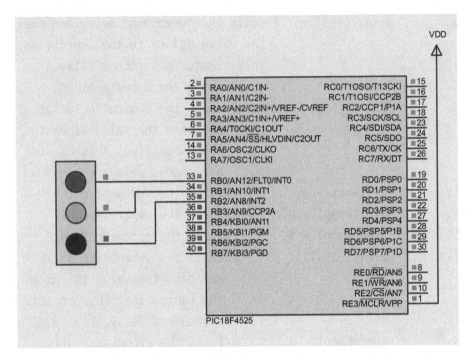

*Figure 4-2.* *The Proteus Simulation of North–South Traffic Lights*

The following sections provide analysis and instructions to explain how the program works.

# The Configuration Words

I should point out that the same configuration words have to be placed in the 'c' file as always and so does the include <xc.h>. This must be included in all your projects.

The configuration words are very important as they define how the PIC sets up its main properties. The most important of which is the primary oscillator source. All the PICs you will come across can use a variety of different oscillator sources from the slow external RC, resistor–capacitor, oscillator to very high-frequency 19.08Mhz external crystal oscillator; note that newer PICs can run at much higher frequencies.

Most PICs also have an internal oscillator block of circuitry that can be used as the primary oscillator source. I prefer to use this internal oscillator block as it saves on the cost of a crystal and saves on available I/O, as there is no need to use RA6 and RA7 as inputs for the external oscillator circuit. However, you may want to do otherwise, so you should appreciate that these configuration words have to be used, and you should know how to set them up. An example of setting these configuration words is explained in Chapter 2.

# The Analysis of the Program

The following is an analysis of the Listing 4-1. Each new instruction will be looked at to explain how they work and what they are trying to do.

Line 1

This is when the directive #define is explained. This directive allows the programmer to create a phrase that can represent a single program instruction or a series of instructions. They can be likened to macros in other programs. Note that these defines are not instructions for the program; they are directives for the compiler. Therefore, there is no need for the semicolon at the end of the definition.

In line 2 the directive is

#define redlamp PORTBbits.RB0

This tells the compiler software that wherever it sees the phrase redlamp, it really means the instruction PORTBbits.RB0. So when the compiler sees the instruction redlamp = 1;

the compiler knows we mean make bit 0 of PORTB a logic '1', and so turn on whatever is connected to it.

Note that MPLABX uses different colors to help identify the different types of keywords. The default color for the directive "#define" is light green, and the default color for the phrase, in this case "redlamp", is light blue. These colors should become evident when using the IDE editor in MPLABX.

The same concept is used in lines 3 and 4 except that the phrases are linked to different bits on PORTB. The idea is to makes the program more readable. However, there is also another advantage in that if we wanted to change the allocation list and connect the lamps to PORTD, we need only make the changes here at the definitions rather than search for every occurrence of the I/O in the program. Much more efficient programming.

At line 5, I am simply using comments to split the program listing up into different sections. Here we are going to declare any variables the program will use. Note that when we declare a variable, we are simply reserving an area in memory where we can store data. The size of the area reserved depends upon the data type we are using. We give the variable a name so that we can refer to it in the program. These variables will be global in that they can be used anywhere in the program. This is opposed to local variables which can only be used in the subroutine that they are declared in.

In line 6 we simply reserve a global variable that is an 8-bit memory location referred to as 'n.' This is an unsigned char which means all 8 bits are used to represent the number from 0 to 255. There can be no negative numbers.

Line 7 simply splits the listing up into a section for any subroutines we want to create.

Line 8 declares a subroutine called "delay". The word void means it does not pass any data back down to the main program. Inside the normal brackets, the subroutine declares a local variable of type unsigned char named "t". This variable is only valid for use inside this subroutine.

Line 9 sets up the opening curly bracket for this subroutine.

Line 10 declares a for do loop. Inside the bracket is makes the variable n = 0; it then asks if n<t; if it is less than 't', then the micro must carry out the instructions inside the curly brackets that follow. It will automatically increment 'n' after it has carried out the instructions inside the curly brackets. It will then ask the question, is n < t? When 'n' is not less than 't', the micro will break out of the for do loop. Note that when the programmer calls this subroutine "delay," it will have to pass a value that will be loaded into the local variable 't'. In this way this delay becomes a variable delay whose length of delay depends upon the value passed up to it which is then loaded into the variable 't'. However, you should appreciate that the largest value you can assign to the local variable 't' is 255. This is because it is an 8-bit memory location.

Line 11 sets up the opening curly bracket for this for do loop.

Line 12 simply loads the value '0' into the TMR0 register. This is so that the TMR0 starts to count from 0.

Line 13 states that while Timer0 is less than 255, do nothing. This creates a 33-ms delay with Timer0 counting at 7812.5Hz one tick = 128us, that is, 256 x 128us = 32.77ms.

Line 14 is the closing curly bracket of the for do loop.

Line 15 is the closing curly bracket of the for the delay subroutine.

Line 16 declares the main loop. This is where the micro goes to get the very first instruction of the program.

Line 17 sets up the opening curly bracket for the main loop.

Lines 18 to 22 simply make sure that all the ports are at logic '0' on all their bits. This is to make sure nothing is turned on by accident.

Line 23 makes sure that all the bits in the SFR, Special Function Register, TRISB are at logic '0.' This makes all bits in PORTB output.

This program only uses PORTB, so we are not bothered about the other TRIS SFRs.

Line 24 makes all the bits in SFR ADCON0 go to logic '0.' This keeps the ADC connected to channel '0' but more important is that it turns the ADC off as we are not using it.

Line 25 makes the bits in the ADCON1 SFR go to 0b00001111. It is bits 3, 2, 1, and 0 that have been set to logic '1' that makes all the inputs digital and not analogue.

Line 26 sets the internal oscillator to 8Mhz and makes it stable.

Line 27 turns Timer0 on. It makes it an 8-bit timer with a maximum divide rate which means it counts at a rate of 7812.5Hz making one tick = 128µS.

Line 28 declares a forever loop as the test inside the while brackets will always be true as it is always a logic '1'. This means the micro will carry out the instructions inside the following curly brackets forever. This is to stop the micro from carrying out the instructions from line 17 to 26 again.

Line 29 sets up the opening curly bracket of the forever loop.

Line 30 turns on the redlamp.

Line 31 calls the delay subroutine and passes the number 153 to be loaded into the local variable 't' in the subroutine. This creates a 5-second delay.

Line 32 turns on the amberlamp.

Line 33 calls a 2-second delay.

Line 34 turns off the redlamp.

Line 35 turns off the amberlamp.

Line 36 turns on the greenlamp.

Line 37 calls the 5-second delay.

Line 38 turns off the greenlamp.

Line 39 turns on the amberlamp.

Line 40 calls the 2-second delay.

Line 41 turns off the amberlamp. As this is the last instruction in this forever loop, the micro goes back to line 30, via lines 28 and 29, to start the process again.

Line 42 is the closing curly bracket of the forever loop.

Line 43 is the closing curly bracket of the for the main loop.

I hope this explains how the program works and what each instruction is doing. With respect to future program listings, I will analyze only the new instructions. In this way I hope you will be able to learn how all the instructions we use in these programs work.

# Downloading the Program to a Prototype Board

It would be useful at this point to show you how to download your program to an actual PIC on a prototype board. There are a range of prototype boards you can use. One that I use for my programs is from Microchip, and it is the PIC Demo board. To connect to the board, I normally use the ICD3 can. These can be found on the Microchip web site. However, to use any programming tool, you must specify which hardware tool you want to use as shown in Figure 2-6, when you create your project in the first place. However, if you have already created your project, you can change the hardware tool by right clicking the project name in the project view tree. You should then see a fly-out window appear from which you can select the word Properties. After selecting Properties, you will be presented with a pop-up window as shown in Figure 4-3.

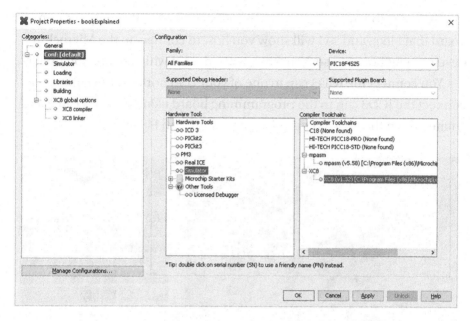

***Figure 4-3.*** *The Properties Window for an Existing Project*

Having made sure you have selected your programming tool and connected to your prototype board, you can download the program to the PIC by clicking the green down arrow from the main menu bar as shown in Figure 4-4. Note that when we were using the simulator tool, these two arrows were not available to us before.

***Figure 4-4.*** *The Downloading to the PIC*

The following picture should help show how to connect the ICD3 can to the PIC prototype board and the laptop. I use two types of prototype boards, one from Matrix Multimedia and one from Microchip. However,

Matrix seems to have moved away from their versatile PIC programming board that I like, and so I will show you how to connect to the Microchip development board I use. You will have to decide which board you prefer.

You connect the ICD3 can to one of your USB ports on the laptop, and connect the ICD3 can to the programming board using the RJ11 cable and connector on the board. This principle is shown in Figure 4-5.

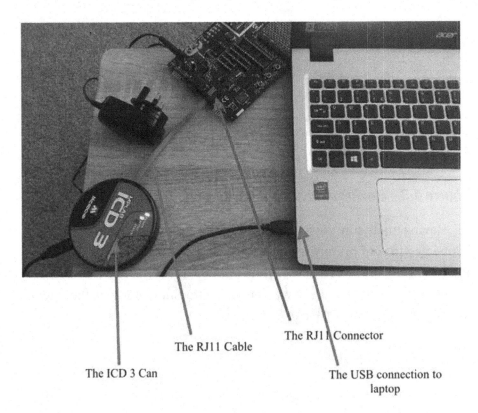

The RJ11 Connector

The RJ11 Cable

The ICD 3 Can

The USB connection to laptop

***Figure 4-5.***  *Downloading to a Prototype Board*

From now on the programs in the book will be simulated with the use of the ECAD software PROTEUS. Those who use PROTEUS may be aware that you can write your PIC programs in PROTEUS as well as use their extensive debugging tools. This book will not go into that aspect of using PROTEUS as that is a book in itself.

# Extending the Program to the Crossroads Traffic Lights

The natural extension to this program would be to write a program that models the full crossroads set of traffic lights, that is, both the North South and the East West set of lights. The timing sequence for this task is as follows (note that N/S lamps are numbered Red1, Amber1, and Green1, whereas E/W are numbered Red2, Amber2, and Green2):

1. The sequence starts with both red lamps on.

2. Five seconds later, Amber1 comes on as well.

3. Two seconds later, Red1 and Amber1 go out, and Green1 comes on.

4. Five seconds later, Green1 goes out, and Amber1 comes back on by itself.

5. Two seconds later, Amber1 goes out, and Red1 comes back on. Note that all this time, Red2 has been on.

6. One second later, Amber2 comes on as well.

7. Two seconds later, Red2 and Amber2 go out, and Green2 comes on.

8. Five seconds later, Green2 goes out, and Amber2 comes back on by itself.

9. Two seconds later, Amber2 goes out, and Red2 comes back on. Note that all this time, Red1 has been on.

10. The cycle now repeats.

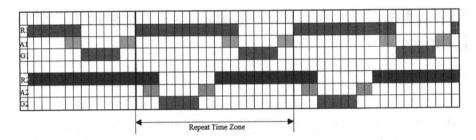

***Figure 4-6.*** *The Timing Diagram for the Crossroads Traffic Lights*

# The Algorithm

The diagram shown in Figure 4-6 was created from the sequence for the traffic lights. Each of the rectangles represents one second in time. Once the timing diagram had been created, it became clear that the 20-second period shown as repeat time zone was, as its name suggest, repeated every 20 seconds. This then means that the only sequence that needed to be programmed was the sequence listed between this repeat time zone periods.

The next step was to list all the important time steps and what we need to have happen at those times. The list is as shown below:

- Time 0. This is the start time in the sequence, and at this time, both Red1 and Red2 should come on.

- Time 1. This is one second later, and at this time, Amber2 should come.

- Time 2. This is two seconds after time 1, and at this time, Amber2 and Red2 should go out, and Green2 should turn on.

- Time 3. This is five seconds after time2, and at this time, Green2 turns off, and Amber2 comes back on again.

110

- Time4. This is 2 seconds after time3, and at this time Amber2 turns off, and Red2 turns back on again.

- Time5. This is 1 second after time4, and at this time, Amber1 is turned on

- Time 6. This is 2 seconds after time5, and this is when Red1, which has been lit all this time, is turned off and Amber1 turns off as well as Green1 is turned on.

- Time 7. This is 5 seconds after time6; at this time Green1 turns off, and Amber1 turns back on again.

- Time 8. This is 2 seconds after time7, and at this time, Amber1 turns off, and the cycle goes back to time0 and starts to repeat the whole sequence.

The program has to create these time steps and turn on and off the appropriate lights at those times.

The program needs 6 outputs to connect the 6 lamps t. Note that there will actually be 12 lamps, but the north and south work together and so does the east and west lamps.

There is no real need for an input, but we will include a start switch that starts the whole sequence.

The program will make use of a variable delay to create the various time steps.

The next step is to draw the flowchart shown in Figure 4-7.

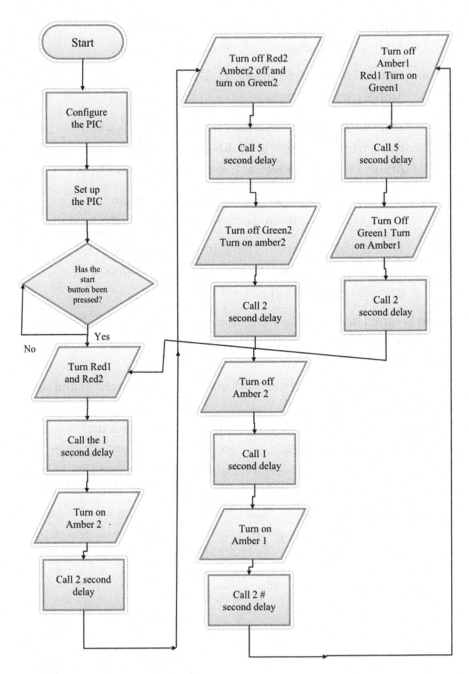

***Figure 4-7.*** *The Flowchart for the Crossroads Traffic Light Program*

The program listing for the crossroads traffic light is shown in Listing 4-2.

***Listing 4-2.*** The Crossroads Traffic Lights

```
1.   #define red1        PORTBbits.RB0    //defines the
                                            symbolic name
                                            red1 to mean bit
                                            0 of PORTB
2.   #define amber1      PORTBbits.RB1    //defines the
                                            symbolic name
                                            amber1 to mean
                                            bit 1 of PORTB
3.   #define green1      PORTBbits.RB2    //defines the
                                            symbolic name
                                            green1 to mean
                                            bit 2 of PORTB
4.   #define red2    PORTBbits.RB3        //defines the
                                            symbolic name
                                            red2 to mean bit
                                            3 of PORTB
5.   #define amber2  PORTBbits.RB4        //defines the
                                            symbolic name
                                            amber2 to mean
                                            bit 4 of PORTB
6.   #define green2  PORTBbits.RB5        //defines the
                                            symbolic name
                                            green2 to mean
                                            bit 5 of PORTB
7.   #define startButton PORTAbits.RA0    //defines the
                                            symbolic name
                                            startButton to
                                            mean bit 0 of
                                            PORTA
```

8.    //Global variables                      //These are variables for
                                               anywhere in the program

9.    unsigned char n;                         //This reserves a memory
                                               location for the 8 bit
                                               variable 'n' using all 8
                                               bits for the number

10.    //Subroutine

11.    void delay(unsigned char t)                     //This is the start
                                                       of a subroutine
                                                       called delay. It
                                                       expects a value to
                                                       be passed up to the
                                                       subroutine which
                                                       it copies into the
                                                       local variable 't'.

12.    {                                        //opening curly bracket of
                                                delay subroutine

13.    for (n = 0; n < t; n++)                  //sets up a for do loop which
                                                controls how many times
                                                the micro carries out the
                                                instructions inside the
                                                curly brackets.

14.    {                                        //opening curly bracket for
                                                the for do loop

15.    TMRO = 0;                                //set TMRO to 0. start value
                                                for count

16.    while (TMRO < 255);                      //while value of TMRO is
                                                less than 255 do nothing.
                                                Lines 15 and 16 create a
                                                32.77msec delay

17.    }                                        //closing curly bracket for
                                                the for do loop

```
18.  }                          //closing curly bracket for
                                   the delay subroutine
19.  void main()                //start of the main loop
20.  {                          //opening curly bracket for
                                   main loop
21.  PORTA = 0;                 //these few lines turn off
                                   all bits on the PORTS
22.  PORTB = 0;
23.  PORTC = 0;
24.  PORTD = 0;
25.  PORTE = 0;
26.  TRISA = 0X0F;              //This makes the first four
                                   bits on PORTA input and the
                                   last four bits are output
27.  TRISB = 0;                 //This sets all bits on PORTB
                                   as outputs
28.  ADCON0 = 0;                //turn ADC off
29.  ADCON1 = 0x0F;             //make all bits digital
30.  OSCCON = 0x74;             //set osc to 8Mhz with stable
                                   output
31.  T0CON = 0xC7;              //set TMR0 to 8 bit reg with
                                   divide by 256 rate so runs
                                   at 7812.5 Hz one tick =
                                   128uS
32.  while (!startButton);      //wait for start Button to be
                                   pressed
33.  while (1)                  //start of the for ever loop
                                   so micro only carries out
                                   lines 19 to 32 only once
34.  {                          //Opening curly bracket for
                                   while loop
```

```
35.  red1 = 1;            //turn red1 on
36.  red2 = 1;            //turn red2 on
37.  delay (30);          //wait 1 second
38.  amber2 = 1;          //turn amber2 on
39.  delay (61);          //wait 2 seconds
40.  red2 = 0;            //turn red2 off
41.  amber2 = 0;          //turn amber2 off
42.  green2 = 1;          //turn green2 on
43.  delay (153);         //wait 5 seconds
44.  green2 = 0;          //turn green2 off
45.  amber2 = 1;          //turn amber2 off
46.  delay(61);           //wait 2 seconds
47.  amber2 = 0;          //turn amber2 off
48.  red2 = 1;            //turn red2 on
49.  delay (30);          //wait 1 second
50.  amber1 = 1;          //turn amber1 on
51.  delay (61);          //wait 2 seconds
52.  red1 = 0;            //turn red1 off
53.  amber1 = 0;          //turn amber1 off
54.  green1 = 1;          //turn green1 on
55.  delay(153);          //wait 5 seconds
56.  green1 = 0;          //turn green1 off
57.  amber1 = 1;          //turn amber1 on
58.  delay(61);           //wait 2 seconds
59.  amber1 = 0;          //turn amber1 off
60.  }
61.  }
```

The circuit for the simulation is shown in Figure 4-8.

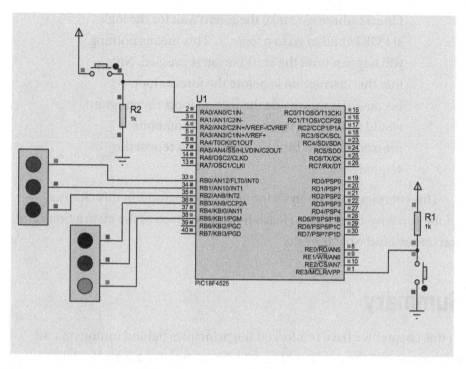

*Figure 4-8.* *The Simulated Crossroads Circuit*

## The Program Analysis

With program Listing 4-2, there are only three new instructions. They are

> Line 7 where we define the phrase startButon to mean the input at PORTAbits.RA0.

> Line 26 where we declare that TRISA = 0X0F; this makes the first four bits in PORTA inputs and the remaining four bits are outputs.

117

Line 32 where we make the micro wait for the logic
at PORTAbit0 to go to a logic '1.' This means nothing
will happen until the start button is pressed. Note
that this instruction is before the forever loop
because if it was inside the forever loop, the program
would wait at this instruction, until someone
pressed the start button, before it can repeat the
sequence.

This completes the analysis for both the programs in this chapter.
I hope you have been able to learn how to use each of the instructions and
you understand what they do.

# Summary

In this chapter we have reinforced the principles behind tuning on and
off outputs and the concept of how to create and use a variable delay
subroutine. We have seen how useful these subroutines are in saving
repeating instructions. This then saves on program memory. In the next
chapter, we learn about the ADC and how to use analogue inputs.

# CHAPTER 5

# Real-World Inputs

In this chapter we will look at using the PIC to measure real-world signals such as signals from pressure, temperature, and speed. It will cover using the three registers that control the ADC and receiving an analogue input and displaying it as a binary value.

After reading this chapter, you will be able to use analogue inputs.

## Using Analogue Inputs

As well as digital inputs, which are usually just on or off, 5v or 0V, PICs can use analogue inputs. These are inputs that can ideally take up any voltage within the range of the PIC, normally any voltage between 0 and 5V. I say ideally because the voltage will increase in discrete steps according to the resolution of the ADC. There is one ADC in the PIC and it is a 10-bit ADC. If the range of voltage is the normal 0 to 5v, then knowing the resolution of the ADC can be calculated using;

$$resolution = \frac{range}{2^n}$$ Equation 1 Resolution of An ADC where 'n' is the number of bits of the ADC

The resolution of the ADC is

$$\therefore resolution = \frac{range}{2^n} = \frac{5}{2^{10}} = \frac{5}{1024} = 4.883mV$$ Equation 2 Resolution of 10 bit ADC

© Hubert Henry Ward 2020
H. H. Ward, *C Programming for the PIC Microcontroller*,
https://doi.org/10.1007/978-1-4842-5525-4_5

What this means is that the ADC will see 0V, and then the next higher voltage will be 4.883mV, and the next would be 9.766mv, and so on. Therefore, the PIC cannot really see every possible voltage from 0 to 5V. However, the result will be close enough for us humans.

The fact that the PIC can use analogue inputs, indeed the PIC18f4525 has up to 13 analogue inputs available to it, means we as programmers must learn how to use them. There are three control registers that control how we use the ADC inputs. They are

- ADCON0

- ADCON1

- ADCON2

## The ADCON0 Control Register

The main purpose of this control register is to allow the programmer to choose which analogue input, or channel, is connected to the ADC. Note that this is a form of multiplexing where many inputs feed into one device one at a time. The choice is controlled by the data in bits 5, 4, 3, and 2 of the ADCON0 register; see Table 5-1. Note that bits 7 and 6 are not used, so they are set to logic '0'.

*Table 5-1.* *The ADCON0 Register (See Data Sheet)*

| Bit 7 | Bit 6 | Bit 5 | Bit 4 | Bit 3 | Bit 2 | Bit 1 | Bit 0 |
|---|---|---|---|---|---|---|---|
| Not Used | Not Used | CHS3 | CHS2 | CHS1 | CHS0 | GO/DONE | ADON |
| Bit 7 | | Not Used read as 0 | | | | | |
| Bit 6 | | Not Used read as 0 | | | | | |

(*continued*)

***Table 5-1.*** (*continued*)

| Bit 7 | Bit 6 | Bit 5 | Bit 4 | Bit 3 | Bit 2 | Bit 1 | Bit 0 |
|-------|-------|-------|-------|-------|-------|-------|-------|
| Bits 5 to Bit 2 | | Bit 5 | Bit 4 | Bit 3 | Bit 2 | ADC Channel Selected | |
| | | 0 | 0 | 0 | 0 | Channel 0 AN0 | |
| | | 0 | 0 | 0 | 1 | Channel 1 AN1 | |
| | | 0 | 0 | 1 | 0 | Channel 2 AN2 | |
| | | 0 | 0 | 1 | 1 | Channel 3 AN3 | |
| | | 0 | 1 | 0 | 0 | Channel 4 AN4 | |
| | | 0 | 1 | 0 | 1 | Channel 5 AN5 | |
| | | 0 | 1 | 1 | 0 | Channel 6 AN6 | |
| | | 0 | 1 | 1 | 1 | Channel 7 AN7 | |
| | | 1 | 0 | 0 | 0 | Channel 8 AN8 | |
| | | 1 | 0 | 0 | 1 | Channel 9 AN9 | |
| | | 1 | 0 | 1 | 0 | Channel 10 AN10 | |
| | | 1 | 0 | 1 | 1 | Channel 11 AN11 | |
| | | 1 | 1 | 0 | 0 | Channel 12 AN12 | |
| | | 1 | 1 | 0 | 1 | Not Used | |
| | | 1 | 1 | 1 | 0 | Not Used | |
| | | 1 | 1 | 1 | 1 | Not Used | |

BIT 1          1 Start a conversion, and a conversion is now taking place
                  0 A conversion has finished

BIT 0          1 Enable the ADC
                  0 Disable the ADC

121

Bit 0 is the bit that actually turns the ADC on or not. A logic '1' means the ADC is enabled, whereas a logic '0' means it is disabled.

The last remaining bit, bit 1, is used to start the ADC conversion and tell the programmer when the conversion is finished or done. The programmer must set this bit to a logic 1 to start the ADC conversion. Then when the conversion is finished, the microprocessor sets this bit back to a logic '0' automatically. This is a signal to tell the programmer the ADC conversion has finished.

# The ADCON1 Register

This register mostly controls whether the 13 inputs are to be used as analogue or digital. It is the first four bits, b0, b1, b2, and b3, that do this. Table 5-2 clearly shows how this is achieved.

*Table 5-2. The ADCON1 Register (See Data Sheet)*

| Bit 7 | Bit 6 | Bit 5 | Bit 4 | Bit 3 | Bit 2 | Bit 1 | Bit 0 |
|---|---|---|---|---|---|---|---|
| Not Used | Not Used | VCFG1 | VCFG0 | PCFG3 | PCFG2 | PCFG1 | PCFG0 |

| Bit 7 | Not Used read as 0 |
|---|---|
| Bit 6 | Not Used read as 0 |
| Bit 5 | 1 negative reference from AN2 |
|  | 0 negative reference from VSS |
| Bit 4 | 1 positive reference from AN3 |
|  | 0 positive reference from VDD |

*(continued)*

***Table 5-2.*** (*continued*)

| B3 | B2 | B1 | B0 | AN12 | AN11 | AN10 | AN9 | AN8 | AN7 | AN6 | AN5 | AN4 | AN3 | AN2 | AN1 | AN0 |
|----|----|----|----|------|------|------|-----|-----|-----|-----|-----|-----|-----|-----|-----|-----|
| 0 | 0 | 0 | 0 | A | A | A | A | A | A | A | A | A | A | A | A | A |
| 0 | 0 | 0 | 1 | A | A | A | A | A | A | A | A | A | A | A | A | A |
| 0 | 0 | 1 | 0 | A | A | A | A | A | A | A | A | A | A | A | A | A |
| 0 | 0 | 1 | 1 | D | A | A | A | A | A | A | A | A | A | A | A | A |
| 0 | 1 | 0 | 0 | D | D | A | A | A | A | A | A | A | A | A | A | A |
| 0 | 1 | 0 | 1 | D | D | D | A | A | A | A | A | A | A | A | A | A |
| 0 | 1 | 1 | 0 | D | D | D | D | A | A | A | A | A | A | A | A | A |
| 0 | 1 | 1 | 1 | D | D | D | D | D | A | A | A | A | A | A | A | A |
| 1 | 0 | 0 | 0 | D | D | D | D | D | D | A | A | A | A | A | A | A |
| 1 | 0 | 0 | 1 | D | D | D | D | D | D | D | A | A | A | A | A | A |
| 1 | 0 | 1 | 0 | D | D | D | D | D | D | D | D | A | A | A | A | A |
| 1 | 0 | 1 | 1 | D | D | D | D | D | D | D | D | D | A | A | A | A |
| 1 | 1 | 0 | 0 | D | D | D | D | D | D | D | D | D | D | A | A | A |
| 1 | 1 | 0 | 1 | D | D | D | D | D | D | D | D | D | D | D | A | A |
| 1 | 1 | 1 | 0 | D | D | D | D | D | D | D | D | D | D | D | D | A |
| 1 | 1 | 1 | 1 | D | D | D | D | D | D | D | D | D | D | D | D | D |

The ADC needs a reference voltage to help determine the level of the analogue input. Bits 4 controls where the PIC gets the positive reference. The default, and so normal setting, is to use the supply to the PIC, that is, VCC or VDD.

Bit 5 controls where the PIC gets the negative reference. The default, and so normal setting, is to use the supply to the PIC, that is, VSS or ground.

Bits 6 and 7 are not used.

# The ADCON2 Register

The ADCON2 control register is used to firstly decide what format the result of the ADC is stored in (Table 5-3). This is because the ADC returns a 10-bit binary number as the result of a conversion. The problem is that this PIC is an 8-bit PIC which means it only has 8-bit registers. This means that the PIC uses two registers to store the result: ADRESH and ADRESL. Therefore 8 bits of the result can be stored in one register; the other 2 bits are stored in the other register.

***Table 5-3.*** *The ADCON2 Register (See Data Sheet)*

| Bit 7 | Bit 6 | Bit 5 | Bit 4 | Bit 3 | Bit 2 | Bit 1 | Bit 0 |
|---|---|---|---|---|---|---|---|
| ADFM | Not Used | ACQT2 | ACQT1 | ACQT0 | ADCS2 | ADCS1 | ADCS0 |

| BIT 7 | 1 Right justify 2 bits in ADRESH (b1 b0) 8 bits in ADRESL |
|---|---|
| | 0 Left justify 8 bits in ADRESH 2 bits in ADRESL (b7 b6) |

| BIT 6 | Not used |
|---|---|

| Bit 5 - Bit 3 | BIT 5 | BIT 4 | BIT 3 | **Selected TADs** |
|---|---|---|---|---|
| | 0 | 0 | 0 | 0 TAD |
| | 0 | 0 | 1 | 2 TAD |
| | 0 | 1 | 0 | 4 TAD |
| | 0 | 1 | 1 | 6 TAD |
| | 1 | 0 | 0 | 8 TAD |
| | 1 | 0 | 1 | 12 TAD |
| | 1 | 1 | 0 | 16 TAD |
| | 1 | 1 | 1 | 20 TAD |

(*continued*)

***Table 5-3.*** (*continued*)

| Bit 7 | Bit 6 | Bit 5 | Bit 4 | Bit 3 | Bit 2 | Bit 1 | Bit 0 |
|-------|-------|-------|-------|-------|-------|-------|-------|
| BIT 2 - BIT0 | | BIT 2 | BIT 1 | BIT 0 | **AD Clock Select Bits** | | |
| | | 0 | 0 | 0 | FOsc/2 | | |
| | | 0 | 0 | 1 | FOsc/8 | | |
| | | 0 | 1 | 0 | FOsc/32 | | |
| | | 0 | 1 | 1 | FRC (RC Clock) | | |
| | | 1 | 0 | 0 | FOsc/4 | | |
| | | 1 | 0 | 1 | FOsc/16 | | |
| | | 1 | 1 | 0 | FOsc/64 | | |
| | | 1 | 1 | 1 | FRC (RC Clock) | | |

The diagram shown in Figure 5-1 helps to explain what is meant by right and left justification.

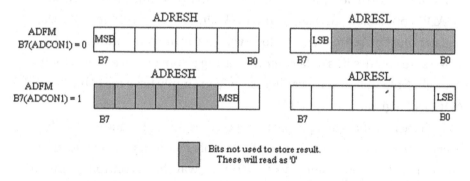

***Figure 5-1.*** *The Storing of the 10-bit Result of the ADC Conversion*

The top diagram where the ADFM or B7 is a logic '0' is termed left justification. Right justification is shown in the bottom diagram. I normally choose left justification.

To understand the other use of the ADCON2 control register, you need to appreciate what has to happen when you turn the ADC on and try to get an ADC conversion result.

When you start a conversion, the PIC will connect the ADC to the particular input, or ADC channel, that is measuring the physical analogue input. Then, once the ADC is connected to the input, it will use the voltage at that input to charge up a capacitor in what is termed a sample and hold circuit. It will take a finite time for the capacitor to charge up to the voltage at that input. This charge up will depend upon the value of the capacitor in the sample and hold circuit and the resistance at the input. This will change depending upon the particular PIC you are using. For the 18F4525 the capacitor has a value of 25pF; see Section 19 in the data sheet. Using this value, an approximate acquisition time for the capacitor to charge up is 2.4μs; see Section 19 in the data sheet.

This basically means you must get the PIC to wait this 2.4μs before the ADC starts its conversion; if it doesn't wait this time, then the result could be inaccurate. Microchip offer two ways of creating this delay. You could manually create a delay routine that you run every time before you start an ADC conversion. To use this method, bits 5, 4, and 3 of the ADCON2 register must be set to logic '0'. However, you as the programmer, must make sure you use this delay before starting a conversion and it is long enough. Note that to start a conversion, you simply have to set bit 1 of the ADCON2 register to a logic '1'.

Microchip offers an approach that creates this delay automatically every time you start a conversion. To use this method, you need to know the period 'T' of the frequency of the timing waveform controlling the ADC conversion process. Microchip calls this period the "TAD". Microchip offers a variety of options for choosing the frequency of the timing waveform. This is because Microchip offers the user a wide variety of oscillator sources for the PIC. Therefore bits 2, 1, and 0 offer the choice of using the RC oscillator as the timing source for the ADC or dividing the oscillator frequency by 2, 4, 8, 16, 32, or 64. The idea is to create a 2.4-μs delay.

The process is best explained with an example. However, to appreciate what we are trying to create, it would be useful to consider the timing waveform shown in Figure 5-2.

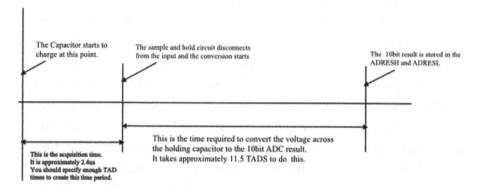

The Capacitor starts to charge at this point.

The sample and hold circuit disconnects from the input and the conversion starts

The 10bit result is stored in the ADRESH and ADRESL

This is the time required to convert the voltage across the holding capacitor to the 10bit ADC result. It takes approximately 11.5 TADS to do this.

This is the acquisition time. It is approximately 2.4us You should specify enough TAD times to create this time period.

**Figure 5-2.**  *The Timing for the ADC Operation of the PIC*

Figure 5-2 depicts what happens when the PIC goes through an ADC conversion. Firstly, the ADC is connected to the relevant analogue input. The voltage at that input is acquired. This means that the input is switched onto the sample and hold circuit inside the PIC and the capacitor in that circuit is charged up to the voltage at the input. This charge-up time is termed the acquisition time, and the PIC must wait long enough for the capacitor to fully charge up. The time that the PIC will wait is set by the chosen number of TAD periods that you, as the programmer, select. You must select enough TAD periods for the capacitor to fully charge up. This then means you must know how long each TAD period is. This is again chosen by you, the programmer.

The TAD period is set using the bits 0, 1, and 2 of the ADCON2 register. These bits are named ADCS0, ADCS1, and ADCS2. With these bits you, can chose the frequency at which the ADC system runs and so the TAD time for the system. Table 5-3 shows the possible selections you can choose. Note the TAD time is equal to the periodic time 'T' of the chosen frequency you select using bits 0, 1, and 2 of the ADCON2 register.

This then means that it is the combination of the number of TADs used to create the acquisition time and the actual TAD period you have chosen that controls how long the PIC waits while the capacitor is allowed to charge up. The one overriding consideration is that the TAD and the minimum number of TADs which is 2TAD must create a time that is equal to or greater than the acquisition time. This means that if the TAD time that you choose worked out to be 500ns and the acquisition time was 2.4µs, then the system could possibly throw up an error as the minimum 2TAD time would 2x500ns = 1µs, not long enough. Of course, you would not choose the 2TAD; you would choose the 6TAD as 6TAD would make the PIC wait 3µs which is greater than the 2.4µs acquisition time for the PIC18F4525. However, you must be aware of the problem.

This is rather a lot to appreciate, and so to help you understand the process, I will go through two examples.

# Creating the Required Acquisition Time

These two examples are to help you appreciate the importance of this acquisition time and how to use and create the TAD time.

The first example is fine as the chosen TAD time is within the specified parameters for the PIC. However, the second example is not recommended as the minimum 2TAD would not produce a long enough acquisition time. Indeed, the minimum divide rate for the 20-Mhz oscillator is divide by 32 as this would give a TAD time of 1.6µS making the minimum 2TAD 3.2µs.

Table 19.1 in the data sheet does give you some suggestion as to the recommended TAD time. However, I must say that Microchip has to give the user the information for the PIC in the data sheet, but they do not make it very clear as to how to use that information.

# Example 1

In this example we will be using the 8-Mhz oscillator, and then choosing a divide by 8 makes the frequency of the ADC operation 1Mhz. This in turn means that the period, known as TAD, is 1µs, that is, $1/1E^6 = 1E^{-6} = 1$µs. Therefore, to create the required acquisition time of 2.4µS, we would need a 2.4TAD time for the delay, that is, $2.4E^{-6}/1E^{-6} = 2.4$.

Using bits 5, 4, and 3 of the ADCON2 register, we have options of using 2, 4, 6, 8, 12, 16, and 20 TAD time period. To obtain the required 2.4µs, you should select the 4 TAD option, the closest to 2.4µs while still be greater then 2.4µs. Note that this 2.4µs is the minimum, not the maximum time the PIC should allow for the acquisition time; however, you should make this delay time the shortest you can.

To select this option, we need to write

- b5 = 0
- b4 = 1
- b3 = 0 4TAD
- b2 = 0
- b1 = 0'
- b0 = 1 divide by 8

# Example 2

In this example we will be using the 20-Mhz oscillator. Then choosing a divide by 4 makes the frequency of the ADC operation 5Mhz. This in turn means that the period, known as TAD, is 200ns. Therefore, to create the required acquisition time of 2.4µS, we would need a 12 TAD time for the delay, that is, $2.4E^{-6}/2E^{-9} = 12$.

Using bits 5, 4, and 3 of the ADCON2 register, we have options of using 2, 4, 6, 8, 12, 16, and 20 TAD time period. To obtain the required 2.4μs, you should select the 16 TAD option. Note that 12 TAD would equal the 2.4μs. However, this 2.4μs is the minimum, not the maximum, and it is safer to make the acquisition time slightly longer than is required. If it is too short, the result may not be accurate enough. To select this option, we need to write

- b5 = 1

- b4 = 1

- b3 = 0 16TAD

- b2 = 1

- b1 = 0'

- b0 = 0 divide by 4

I feel I should also add that the preceding description of how to create and use the TAD time for the ADC is my own interpretation. Although I have found it to work well in all my programs that use the ADC; I cannot guarantee that my interpretation is 100% correct. However, I do think it is. This TAD time is one of the most confusing aspects of the PIC that you as a programmer need to calculate. My interpretation is the best one I have come across, and it makes total sense to me. You must make up your own mind.

# Changing the ADC Input Channels

There is the possibility that you, as the programmer, will ask the ADC to switch to a different channel. This will take a finite amount of time, and even though this may only be few microseconds, you must wait until the ADC has changed channels before starting the ADC conversion. It is the data in the ADCON0 register that determines what channel the ADC is connected to; see Table 5-1.

# A Basic Setup for the ADC

I believe it is better to use left justification, B7 = logic '0', as this means that the two least significant bits are stored in ADRESL; see Figure 5-1. For all but the most accurate uses, the programmer can ignore these two bits as they only represent voltages from 0 to 20mV approximately, at 5mv/bit. Indeed, if you ignore these two bits, it really means that you are using an 8-bit ADC instead of a 10 bit. The resolution then reduces to around 19mV per bit.

Using these three control registers, ADCON0, ADCON1, and ADCON2, it is fairly easy to set the ADC up. As an example, suppose you had an analogue input connected to AN0 or bit 0 of PORTA. Assuming you were using VCC and 0V as the reference for the ADC. To set up the ADC, but not start a conversion yet, you would write the following data to the three control registers. The 10-bit result is stored across two 8-bit registers, ADRESH and ADRESL. We will use left justify for the ADC result, which means the 8 most significant bits go into ADRESH and the 2 least significant bits go into b7 and b6 of ADRESL. We set this by making B7 of ADCON2 a logic '0'. We use the oscillator divide by 8 option and the 4TAD option.

Inside the initialization, we will set up the ADC using the following instructions:

```
ADCON0 = 0x01;    //Enable the ADC and select channel 0 and
                    turn the ADC on.
ADCON1 = 0x0E;    //make all bits digital except RA0.
ADCON2 = 0x11;    // Select 4TAD and divide the oscillator by 8.
```

To start an ADC conversion, we must set bit 1 of the ADCON0 register, the GO bit, to a logic '1'. Then wait until the ADC has finished. This is indicated by bit 1 of the ADCON0 register going low to logic '0'. Note that this will happen automatically once the ADC conversion has finished.

The result will then be in the ADRESH and ADRESL.

# A Basic Program for the ADC

Listing 5-1 is a program that has a variable voltage applied to AN0, that is, channel 0. The program will continually read the voltage at this input and display the binary value from the result of the ADC on eight LEDs connected to PORTB of the PIC.

# The Algorithm

The PIC will use the ADC; therefore, this has to be turned on, and channel 0 must be selected as this is the input that the voltage is connected to.

The PIC will use eight LEDs connected to PORTB.

Therefore, PORTA must be set as inputs with at least RA0 set as analogue the rest could be set as digital.

PORTB must be set as output, and those used as possible analogue should be set as digital.

The program will constantly get the result of the ADC and display it on PORTB.

*Listing 5-1.* The Basic ADC Program

```
1.  void main ()         //The  start of the main loop
2.  {                    //the opening curly bracket of
                           the main loop
3.  PORTA = 0;           //just make sure nothing connected
                           to will be turned on PORTA
4.  PORTB = 0;           //just make sure nothing connected
                           to will be turned on PORTB
5.  TRISA = 0x0f;        //Set b0 to b3 of TRISA to logic
                           '1' making them inputs, Set
                           rest to logic '0' making them
                           outputs
```

```
6.    TRISB = 0x00;            //Set all bits in TRISB to
                               logic'0' making all in PORTB
                               outputs.
7.    OSCCON = 0x74;           //set osc to 8Mhz with stable
                               output
8.    ADCON0 = 0x01;           //Turn the ADC on and select
                               channel 0.
9.    ADCON1 = 0x0E;           //Make all bits digital except
                               RA0 which will be analogue.
10.         ADCON2 = 0b00010001;     //Select left justify
                               and 4TAD and divide
                               oscillator by 8
11.         while (1)          // Always do what is within the
                               following curly brackets.
12.         {                  //the opening curly bracket of
                               the forever loop
13.    ADCON0bits.GO_DONE = 1; //Start the ADC conversion
14.    while (ADCON0bits.GO_DONE ==1);  //Do nothing until
                               the conversion
                               has finished
15.         PORTB = ADRESH;         //Write the contents of
                               ADRESH to PORTB so PORTB
                               displays the result of
                               the conversion.
16.         }                  //The closing curly brackets
                               of the forever loop
17.         }                  //The closing curly bracket
                               of the main loop
```

Note that the normal configuration words and the include directives have been included in the project but are not shown here.

The circuit created in PROTEUS is shown in Figure 5-3.

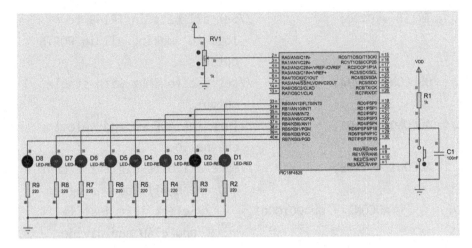

***Figure 5-3.*** *The Simulation Circuit for the Basic ADC*

# Analysis of the Program

Most of the instructions have already been analyzed with Listing 4-1. Therefore, I will only look at the new instructions. These are as follows.

Line 9 Here the ADCON1 SFR is loaded with 0x0E. This is the binary number 0b00001110. It is the four bits 0, 1, 2, and 3 that determine if the inputs are digital or analogue. If you examine Table 5-1, you will see that this combination makes all inputs digital except bit 0 of PORTA. This is set to analogue.

Line 13 Here we set the bit 1 of the ADCON2 SFR to a logic '1'. This will tell the PIC to start an ADC conversation after the PIC has waited the specified number of TAD periods.

Line 14 Here we tell the PIC to do nothing, while bit 1 of the ADCON2 SFR is a logic '1'. This makes the program wait until the ADC conversion has finished. Note that when the ADC completes, the PIC will automatically reset bit 1 of the ADCON2 SFR back to a logic '0' and load the result of the ADC into the ADRESH and ADRESL according to the justification we chose with bit 7 of the SFR ADCON2.

Line 15 All we do here is load the output PORT, PORTB, with a copy of the data that has been loaded into the ADRESH as a result of the ADC operation. As we have chosen left justification, this will be the 8 most significant bits of the ADC result.

I hope this analysis is sufficient for you to understand the program instructions. You should now feel confident in using the ADC inside the PIC.

# Summary

In this chapter we have learnt how to set up the ADC, analogue to digital Converter. We have learnt how to use it to measure the analogue signal at one of the PICs inputs and display it on eight LEDs on PORTB.

In the next chapter, we will learn how to set up an LCD, liquid crystal display. Then use that LCD to display the value of an analogue voltage applied to an input on the PIC.

# CHAPTER 6

# Using the LCD

This chapter shows you how to set up the liquid crystal display (LCD) to show text and numbers on it. You'll then create your own characters to be displayed on the LCD. The chapter concludes by reviewing how to use arrays and pointers. At that point, the LCD should display 2 lines of 16 characters. But let's first review how most LCDs work and how the programmer can control them and so use them.

## The LCD Controller

This description will be based around the LM016L LCD.

Most LCDs use either the Samsung KS0066U or Hitachi HD44780 driver which converts your binary digits into the required signals.

The LCD we will use has 2 lines of 16 characters.

The LCD has 8 data lines, but to enable programmers to save I/O, it can be set up to use all 8 data lines or just 4 data lines.

There are two modes of communicating with the LCD, instruction mode and data mode.

## Instruction or Command Mode

This is used to initialize the LCD and then move the cursor positions such:

- Send cursor to line 2.

- Shift cursor to the right or left a number of characters.

© Hubert Henry Ward 2020
H. H. Ward, *C Programming for the PIC Microcontroller*,
https://doi.org/10.1007/978-1-4842-5525-4_6

- Move the cursor 1 bit to the right after each character or not.

- Send the cursor to the home position.

- Clear the screen.

- Blink or not blink the cursor.

# Data Mode

The LCD is programmed to recognize characters using ASCII code for each character. Basically, the LCD has memory locations, which are nonvolatile; the memory keeps the data even when the power is removed, where the pixel information to draw any one of the ASCII characters are stored. The address of each of these pixel maps corresponds to the same address found in the ASCII character standard table shown in Table 6-1. In other words, the address of where the pixel map is stored corresponds to the ASCII for that character.

*Table 6-1.* *The Main ASCII Character Set*

| High Nibble | 0000 | 0010 | 0011 | 0100 | 0101 | 0110 | 0111 |
|---|---|---|---|---|---|---|---|
| Low nibble | CG.Ram Location | | | | | | |
| xxxx 0000 | 1 | | 0 | @ | P | \ | p |
| xxxx 0001 | 2 | ! | 1 | A | Q | a | q |
| xxxx 0010 | 3 | " | 2 | B | R | b | r |
| xxxx 0011 | 4 | # | 3 | C | S | c | s |

*(continued)*

*Table 6-1.* (*continued*)

| High Nibble | 0000 | | 0010 | 0011 | 0100 | 0101 | 0110 | 0111 |
|---|---|---|---|---|---|---|---|---|
| Low nibble | CG.Ram Location | | | | | | | |
| xxxx 0100 | 5 | | $ | 4 | D | T | d | t |
| xxxx 0101 | 6 | | % | 5 | E | U | e | u |
| xxxx 0110 | 7 | | & | 6 | F | V | f | v |
| xxxx 0111 | 8 | | ' | 7 | G | W | g | w |
| xxxx 1000 | 1 | | < | 8 | H | X | h | x |
| xxxx 1001 | 2 | | > | 9 | I | Y | i | y |
| xxxx 1010 | 3 | | * | : | J | Z | j | z |
| xxxx 1011 | 4 | | + | ; | K | [ | k | { |
| xxxx 1100 | 5 | | ' | < | L | | l | l |
| xxxx 1101 | 6 | | - | = | M | ] | m | } |
| xxxx 1110 | 7 | | . | > | N | ^ | n | |
| xxxx 1111 | 8 | | / | ? | O | _ | o | |

Using the table, it can be seen that the 8-bit number that stands for the character '0' is 00110000. Note that the horizontal information along the top of the table is the four bits B7, B6, B5, and B4, that is, the high nibble, while the information along the vertical at the side of the table is the four bits, B3, B2, B1, and B0, the low nibble. For example, the ASCII for the character 'a' is 01100001.

To call up these characters from within the LCD's memory and so display them on the LCD, the programmer has to write the address of where the pixel map is stored in the LCD's memory. The address corresponds to the number in the ASCII character set. This means that to display the number '0', the programmer has to send the address number 00110000 to the LCD. The LCD control program then opens this address where it finds the pixel map for the character '0'. Also, to display the character 'a', they would send the information 01100001 to open up that location and find the pixel map for the letter 'a'.

This level of understanding will be put to good use when we look at creating special characters.

Each set of information, be it data or instructions, must be sent on either all 8 data lines or just 4 data lines. We will use just 4 lines. This means that the info must be sent in two nibbles, the high nibble first followed by the low nibble.

Note that a nibble stands for just 4 bits, whereas a byte stands for 8 bits, and a word stands for 16 bits.

We will connect the LCD to PORTB, but really any port would do except perhaps PORTA as this is used for the analogue inputs.

Data 4 on the LCD goes to b0 on PORTB of the PIC.

Data 5 on the LCD goes to b1 on PORTB of the PIC.

Data 6 on the LCD goes to b2 on PORTB of the PIC.

Data 7 on the LCD goes to b3 on PORTB of the PIC.

Data pins D0 to D3 are not connected as we will set the LCD to 4-bit operation.

The RS pin on the LCD is connected to b4 on PORTB. Note that it is the RS pin on the LCD that is used to distinguish between instructions to the LCD or data to be displayed on the LCD. The RS pin goes to logic '0' for instructions, and the RS pin goes to logic '1' for data to be displayed.

The 'E' pin is connected to b5 on PORTB. This pin should simply go high then low with no time in between. This action is to tell the driver inside the LCD that some new information has been sent to the LCD and it should deal with it.

A variable voltage can be connected to the VEE pin of the LCD to control the contrast of the LCD. However, I find that using two resistors to divide the voltage down to around 300mv works fine.

The R/W pin, which is the Read/Write pin, should be connected to 0v or ground as it is a logic '0' at this pin that tells the driver we want to write to the LCD.

The full pin connection is shown in Figure 6-1.

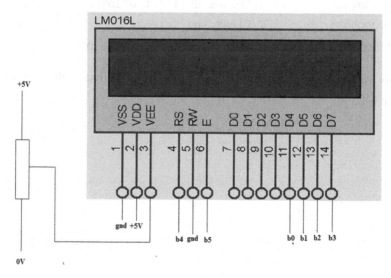

*Figure 6-1. Connecting the LCD*

# Initializing the LCD

We must ensure that power has been applied to the LCD for at least 30ms before we send any information, data, or instruction to the LCD. This is to allow the circuitry of the LCD to settle down and be ready to receive instructions or data.

This can be done using a small LCD delay routine.

Then we can set up the LCD.

To do this we must send the following data in this order:

1. 0b00110011        // First data
2. 0b00110011        // Second data a repeat of the
                     first data
3. 0b00110010        //LCD set up for 4 bit operation
4. 0b00101100        //LCD set up for 2 lines
5. 0b00000110        //Increment the position of the cursor
                     after each character, i.e. move the
                     cursor one place to the right.
6. 0b00001100        //Cursor does not blink
7. 0b00000001        //Clear the screen
8. 0b00000010        //Return cursor to home position.

This information has been derived from the LCD instruction set shown in Table 6-2.

*Table 6-2.* *The LCD Instruction Set*

| Function | B7 | B6 | B5 | B4 | B3 | B2 | B1 | B0 | Execution Time |
|---|---|---|---|---|---|---|---|---|---|
| Clear Screen | 0 | 0 | 0 | 0 | 0 | 0 | 0 | 1 | 1.53ms |
| Description | Clear all display data. It also sends the cursor back to the start of the display. Sets the DDRAM address to 0 | | | | | | | | |
| Return Home | 0 | 0 | 0 | 0 | 0 | 0 | 1 | x | 1.53ms |
| Description | This sends the cursor back to the start of the display. Sets the DDRAM address to 0. The 'x' means it does not care what logic is in that bit | | | | | | | | |
| Entry Mode | 0 | 0 | 0 | 0 | 0 | 1 | I/D | SH | 39μs |
| Description | This sets the cursor movement after entry (I/D); logic '0' in this bit means cursor is decremented; logic '1' means cursor is incremented In the SH bit logic '0' means don't shift the cursor; logic '1' means shift the cursor | | | | | | | | 39μs |
| Display Control | 0 | 0 | 0 | 0 | 1 | D | C | B | 39μs |
| Description | D bit logic '0' display is off logic '1' display is on C bit logic '0' cursor is off Logic '1' cursor is on B bit logic '0' cursor blink is off Logic '1' cursor blink is on | | | | | | | | |
| Cursor/Display Shift | 0 | 0 | 0 | 1 | S/C | R/L | X | x | 39μs |
| Description | S/C bit logic '0' means the cursor is shifted Logic '1' means the display is shifted R/L bit logic '0' means shift left; logic '1' means shift right | | | | | | | | |

*(continued)*

143

*Table 6-2.* (*continued*)

| Function | B7 | B6 | B5 | B4 | B3 | B2 | B1 | B0 | Execution Time |
|---|---|---|---|---|---|---|---|---|---|
| Function Set | 0 | 0 | 0 | 1 | 1 | 0 | X | x | 39μs |
| Description | Configuration data to set up the LCD (Send First) | | | | | | | | |
| Set CGRAM Address | 0 | 1 | A5 | A4 | A3 | A2 | A1 | A0 | |
| Set DDRAM Addess | 1 | A6 | A5 | A4 | A3 | A2 | A1 | A0 | |
| Write Data CGRAM or DDRAM RS Pin Is a Logic '1' | D7 | D6 | D5 | D4 | D3 | D2 | D1 | D0 | 43μs |

To make sure the LCD realizes that this information, being sent to it, is a set of instructions, we must make sure that the RS pin goes low. Note that this means that bit 4 of PORTB must go low.

When using the LCD in 4-bit operation, it is the high nibble that should be sent to the LCD first.

The first 4 bits of PORTB must have the information. This does present a problem in that the four bits, b0, 1, 2, and 3, of information must be sent at the same time as the other bits of PORTB, which includes b4 which is the RS pin. This RS pin must be set to a logic '0' if the information is an instruction or logic '1' if the information is data to be displayed. The process by which this is done is by performing a logic 'OR' operation, with the information waiting to go to the LCD and a variable. We will call this variable rsOR. This must be done before the information is sent to the LCD.

Following is an outline of the process:

1. Consider sending the information to display the character 'b'. The information is 01100010 (Table 6-1).

2. We firstly have to get just the high nibble, that is, '0110'; as we send the high nibble first, then the low nibble.

3. Note that we must save the information, 01100010, as well so that we can get the low nibble later.

4. We then have to make sure that b4 of the information being sent to PORTB is a logic 1. To achieve this, we can create another variable called rsOR. As the information is data to be displayed, we must make sure b4 of the variable rsOR is at logic '1'. Therefore, use the instruction rsOR = 0x10, that is, 0b00010000.

5. Once the data has been sent to the LCD, we must make sure the 'E' pin which is connected to b5 of PORTB goes high then low.

The following set of instructions should achieve this.

```
lcdInfo = 0b01100010;
//this loads lcdInfo with the information for the character 'b'.
lcdTempInfo = lcdInfo;
//This saves a copy of icdInfo in lcdTempInfo
rsOr = 0x10;
//this makes sure bit4 of rsOr is logic '1'
lcdTempInfo = (lcdTempInfo << 4 | lcdTempInfo >>4);
        //this will swap the nibbles around in lcdTempInfo ready
        to send to the LCD after this data in lcdTempInfo =
        0b00100110
lcdInfo = lcdTempInfo & 0x0F;
```

```
// this basically ignores the last four bits of the lcdTempInfo
   b4, b5, b6 and b7 will always be logic '0' and loads the result
   into lcdInfo after this the data in lcdInfo = 0b00000110
lcdInfo = lcdInfo | rsOr;
// This performs a logical OR with lcdInfo and rsOr. This
   allows us to determine if the info is an instruction or data
   after this data in lcdInfo = 0b00010110 i.e. bit 4 is a logic
   '1' the information is data to be displayed on the LCD
lcdPort = lcdInfo;
// this sends the info to the LCD
eBit = 1;
eBit = 0;
// this is to tell the driver that new info has arrived and the
   lcd should deal with it.
```

This is quite a complex set of requirements to understand, but if you read through it a few times, it should help. Also, when you look through the program listing, you should start to understand the process.

Hopefully this goes someway toward explaining how the program can distinguish between sending instructions and data to the LCD.

If the LCD was being used in 8-bit mode, then the RS line and the E line would be connected to another PORT and the corresponding bits of that PORT would have to be set high and low appropriately. Also, there would be no need to split the information up into the high and low nibbles, and OR it as we do with the 4-bit operation.

The reason why we are using the LCD in 4-bit operation is just to save I/O pins. A complete program to use the LCD in 4-bit mode is described in Listing 6-1.

***Listing 6-1.*** The Complete Program for 4bit LCD

```
1.    //Use some comments to try and split the program listing
         up into different sections.
2.    //Create any definitions
```

```
3.    #define firstbyte      0b00110011
4.    #define secondbyte     0b00110011
5.    #define fourBitOp      0b00110010   //this sets the LCD up
                                          for 4 bit operation
                                          instead of 8 bit
6.    #define twoLines       0b00101100   //This sets the LCD to
                                          2 lines mode
7.    #define incPosition    0b00000110   //This tells the LCD to
                                          increment the cursor
                                          position after any
                                          data is displayed
8.    #define cursorNoBlink  0b00001100   //this turns the cursor
                                          off so we don't see
                                          it flashing
9.    #define clearScreen    0b00000001   //this clears the
                                          screen of all display
10.   #define returnHome     0b00000010   //this sends the
                                          cursor back to start
                                          position on the
                                          display
11.   #define lineTwo        0b11000000   //this will send the
                                          cursor to the start
                                          of line 2 on the
                                          display
12.   #define doBlink        0b00001111   //this turns the cursor
                                          on and makes it blink
13.   #define shiftLeft      0b00010000   //this shifts the
                                          cursor one position
                                          to the left
14.   #define shiftRight     0b00010100   //this shifts the
                                          cursor one position
                                          to the right
```

15.  #define lcdPort        PORTB          //this sets which the
                                           LCD is connected to
                                           port

16.  #define eBit        PORTBbits.RB5    //this sets the bit
                                           for the E pin on
                                           the LCD

17.  #define rspin       PORTBbits.RB4    //this sets the bit
                                           for the RS pin on
                                           the LCD

18.        //some variables These comments are just to split the
           listing  up into its logical sections

19.  unsigned char lcdInfo, lcdTempInfo, rsOr;
                                    //this reserves 3 8 bit memory
                                    Locations 1 for  each variable

20.  unsigned char n;              //this reserves an 8 bit
                                    memory location for the
                                    variable 'n'

21.  char str[80];                 //This sets up 80 memory
                                    locations one after
                                    the other in an array.
                                    This array is used for
                                    sending a string to the
                                    LCD

22.  char lcdInitialise [8] =      //This sets up 8 memory
                                    locations in an array
                                    and loads each location
                                    with some initial data
                                    in each location

23.  {                            //The opening bracket of
                                    the array

24. firstbyte,

// note the data in each location is one of the set up instructions for the LCD

25. secondbyte,

//just a repeat of the first byte

26. fourBitOp,

//puts the lcd into 4bit mode not 8 bit

27. twoLines,

//set the lcd up for using two lines of 16 characters

28. incPosition,

//sets the lcd up for moving the cursor one place to the right every time a character is displayed

29. cursorNoBlink,

//sets the lcd up to not show the cursor on the screen

30. clearScreen,

//clears all characters from the lcd display

31. returnHome,

//sends the cursor to the beginning of line 1

32. };

//This is the closing bracket of the array. Note the semi colon is needed as this is the end of a program instruction

33. //the subroutine
34. void sendInfo ()

// a subroutine to send Info to the lcd.

35.  `{`                                    //opening curly bracket of the sendInfo subroutine

36.  `lcdTempInfo = (lcdTempInfo << 4 | lcdTempInfo >>4);`
                                          //this will swap the nibbles around in lcdTempInfo ready to send to the LCD

37.  `lcdInfo = lcdTempInfo & 0x0F;`       // this basically ignores the last four bits of the lcdTempInfo b4, b5, b6  and b7 will always be logic '0'and loads the  result into lcdInfo

38.  `lcdInfo = lcdInfo | rsOr;`           // This performs a logical OR with lcdInfo and rsOr. this allows us to determine if the info is an instruction or data

39.  `lcdPort = lcdInfo;`                  // this sends the info to the LCD

40.  `eBit = 1;`                           // this is to tell the driver that new info has arrived at the lcd

41.  `eBit = 0;`

42.  `TMR0 = 0;`

43.  `while (TMR0 < 16);`                  //this is a 2mS delay at 7812.5Hz long enough for the lcd to process any information see Table 6-2

```
44.  }                              //closing curly bracket
                                    of the sendInfo
                                    subroutine

45.  void lcdOut ()                 //this subroutine gets
                                    the data ready to go to
                                    the sendInfo

46.  {                              //opening curly bracket
                                    of the lcdOut
                                    subroutine

47.  lcdTempInfo = lcdInfo;         // store the information
                                    in a temporary location

48.  sendInfo ();                   //this calls the
                                    subroutine sendInfo to
                                    send the high nibble
                                    first

49.  sendInfo ();                   //this calls the
                                    subroutine sendInfo
                                    again to send  the low
                                    nibble next

50.  }                              //closing curly bracket
                                    of the lcdOut
                                    subroutine

51.  void setUpTheLCD ()            //This is a subroutine to
                                    set up the lcd

52.  {                              //opening curly bracket
                                    of the setUpTheLCD
                                    subroutine

53.  TMR0 = 0; while (TMR0 <255);   //a 32ms delay this is
                                    the time required by
                                    the driver circuit to
                                    settle down
```

54.  n = 0;                              //load the variable 'n'
                                         with the starting value
                                         of 0

55.  rs0r = 0X00;                        // this ensures bit 4
                                         or the RS pin will be
                                         logic '0' as these are
                                         instructions

56.  while (n < 8)                       //while the value in
                                         the variable 'n' is
                                         less than 8 do what
                                         is inside the curly
                                         brackets.

57.  {                                   //the opening bracket for
                                         the while instruction

58.  lcdInfo = lcdInitialise [n];        //load the variable
                                         "lcdInfo" with what is
                                         in location 'n' in the
                                         lcdInitialise array.
                                         As 'n' starts out at 0
                                         this will be the first
                                         location in the array.
                                         See lines 22 to 32
                                         above.

59.  lcdOut ();                          //call the subroutine
                                         lcdOut see lines 45 to
                                         50

60.  n ++;                               //add one to the value
                                         of 'n' the micro will
                                         now go back to line 56.
                                         Note the value of 'n'
                                         will eventually get to
                                         8. When this happens

and the micro goes to line 56 the micro will jump to line 62 after executing line 56 as the condition in the brackets is untrue.

61.  }    //closing curly bracket of the while

62.  rsOr = 0x10;    //this ensures bit 4 of the rsOr is a logic '1' for data

63.  }    //closing curly bracket of setUp subroutine

64.  void line2 ()    // a subroutine to send the cursor of the lcd to the start of line 2

65.  {    //opening curly bracket of Line2 subroutine

66.  rsOr = 0X00;    // this ensures bit 4 or the RS pin will be logic '0' as these are instructions

67.  lcdInfo = lineTwo;    //loads the variable "lcdInfo" with the instruction to send the cursor to  line two

68.  lcdOut ();    //call the subroutine lcdOut

69.  rsOr = 0x10;    //this ensures bit 4 of the rsOr is a logic '1' for data

| | |
|---|---|
| 70.  } | //closing curly bracket of Line2 subroutine |
| 71.  void clearTheScreen () | //a subroutine to clearTheScreen |
| 72.  { | //opening curly bracket for clearTheScreen Subroutine |
| 73.  rsOr = 0X00; | // this ensures bit 4 or the RS pin will be logic '0' as these are instructions |
| 74.  lcdInfo = clearScreen; | //load the variable "lcdInfo" with the instruction to clear the lcd display |
| 75.  lcdOut (); | //call the subroutine "lcdOut" |
| 76.  lcdInfo = returnHome; | //load the variable "lcdInfo" with the instruction to return the cursor to the beginning of line 1 on the lcd display |
| 77.  lcdOut (); | //call the subroutine "lcdOut" |
| 78.  rsOr = 0x10; | //this ensures bit 4 of the rsOr is a logic '1' for data |
| 79.  } | //closing curly bracket of clearScreen subroutine |

```
80.   void writeString (const char *words)    //this is a
                                              subroutine that
                                              will display a
                                              whole string of
                                              characters on
                                              the display.

81.   {                                   //opening curly bracket
                                          for writeString
                                          Subroutine

82.   while (*words)                      // while the *words
                                          pointer is not pointing
                                          to the NULL char do
                                          what is inside the
                                          curly brackets

83.   {                                   //opening curly bracket
                                          for the while

84.   lcdInfo = *words;                   //load what the *words
                                          pointer is pointing
                                          to into the variable
                                          lcdInfo

85.   lcdOut ();                          // call the subroutine to
                                          pass the data to the
                                          LCD

86.   *words ++;                          // increment the contents
                                          of the pointer so that
                                          it is pointing to the
                                          next char in the   array

87.   }                                   //closing curly bracket
                                          for the while

88.   }                                   //closing curly bracket
                                          for the writeString
                                          subroutine
```

```
89.  void main ()
90.  {                              //this is the opening
                                      brackets of the main
                                      loop

91.  PORTA = 0;                     //this makes sure the
                                      PORTS don't turn
                                      anything on

92.  PORTB = 0;
93.  PORTC = 0;
94.  PORTD = 0;
95.  TRISA = 0Xff;                  //set all bits on PORTA
                                      to inputs
96.  TRISB = 0x00;                  //set all bits on PORTB
                                      to outputs
97.  TRISC = 0x00;                  //set all bits on PORTC
                                      to outputs
98.  TRISD = 0x00;                  //set all bits on PORTD
                                      to outputs
99.  ADCON0 = 0b00000001;           //bit 0 = '1' means adc
                                      on bits 5,4,3&2 = '0'
                                      means channel 0 AN0 is
                                      selected
100.      ADCON1 = 0b00001011;      //bits A0 to A3 are
                                      analogue rest are
                                      digital
101.      ADCON2 = 0b00010001;      //select left justify
                                      4TAD Clock = FOSC/8 i.e
                                      1MHz TOSC = 1mS 2.4u/1m
                                      = 2.4 4x1m = 4ms
102.      OSCTUNE = 0x00;           //don't use any of the
                                      fine tuning aspects for
                                      the oscillator
```

```
103.        OSCCON = 0x74;          //this sets the internal
                                      oscillator to 8MHz
                                      stable
104.        TOCON = OXC7;           //this turns timer 0
                                      on, makes it an 8 bit
                                      timer with the maximum
                                      dived  rate
105.        setUpTheLCD ();         //call the subroutine to
                                      set up the LCD
106.        while (1)               //this is the forever
                                      loop to ensure lines 91
                                      to 105 are only carried
                                      out once.
107.        {                       //opening curly bracket
                                      for the forever loop
108.        writeString ("Hello World");  // this sends the
                                              string "Hello World"
                                              to the LCD
109.        line2 ();               //call the subroutine
                                      line2 to move the
                                      cursor to the beginning
                                      of line  two on the LCD
110.        lcdInfo = 0b00110101;   //this is the ascii
                                      character for the
                                      number 5
111.        lcdOut ();              //call the subroutine to
                                      send the number out to
                                      the LCD
112.        lcdInfo = 0b00110111;   //this is the ascii
                                      character for the
                                      number 7
```

| | | |
|---|---|---|
| 113. | lcdOut (); | //call the subroutine to send the number out to the LCD |
| 114. | lcdInfo = 0b00111001; | //this is the ascii character for the number 9 |
| 115. | lcdOut (); | //call the subroutine to send the number out to the LCD |
| 116. | while (1); | //this is another forever loop used to make the program halt at this point as the PIC will for ever do nothing |
| 117. | } | //closing brackets for the first forever loop |
| 118. | } | //this is the closing brackets of the main loop |

Note that the config and include sections of the project are not shown here, but they must be included in the project.

This program listing will introduce a number of different techniques for programming the PICs, all of which make the programming easier to understand and more efficient. However, before we look at those new techniques, we will see how the program performs what is required of it.

The main loop starts at line 89 and ends at line 118. You should understand that the line numbers in the preceding text do not correspond exactly to the line numbers in MPLABX as the configuration and include commands are not shown above. Note how MPLABX links all the lines inside this boundary with a straight line. Line 89 starts with a box, in the editing window of the IDE, inside which is the small '-' minus symbol.

This gives the programmer the ability to close all these groups of lines and shrink them away, thus taking up less room on the editing window. The '-' minus sign is then replaced with '+' plus sign which allows you to expand upon all the lines in the boundary. It is a useful tool if you are confident the lines don't need any editing. This is only visible in the MPLABX editing window, not in the text shown above.

The first few lines up to and including line 105 simply set up the PIC as we want. The define declaration has been explained in program Listing 4-1.

## The Subroutine lcdOut ()

This is between lines 45 and 50 .

Line 47 loads the variable lcdTempInfo with the contents of lcdInfo.

Line 48 calls the subroutine sendInfo () for the first time which will send the high nibble of the information along with the correct value in b4, to the LCD.

Line 49 calls the subroutine sendInfo () for the second time which will send the low nibble of the information along with the correct value in b4, to the LCD.

## The Subroutine sendInfo ()

This is between lines 34 and 44.

Line 36 swaps the 2 nibbles in the variable lcdTempInfo over as we need to send the high nibble first.

Line 37 reloads the variable lcdInfo with the result of the logical AND operation of lcdTempInfo and the binary value 0b00001111. This ensures that b7, b6, b5, and b4 of the result are logic '0's The other four bits are the same as b3, b2, b1, and b0 of lcdTempInfo.

Line 38 performs the logical 'OR' operation of the variables lcdInfo and rsOR. In this instance, because b4 of lcdInfo and b4 of rsOR are both logic '0', then nothing changes as this is an instruction. However, if b4 of

159

rsOR had been changed to a logic '1', then the result would be that b4 of the variable lcdInfo would now go to a logic '1' indicating that the information about to be sent to the LCD was data to be displayed.

Line 39 sends the contents of lcdInfo to PORTB which is the port that the LCD is connected to.

Line 40 sends the 'E' to a logic '1'.

Line 41 sends the 'E' to a logic '0'. The purpose of these two lines are to tell the LCD that it must do something with the information at its data pins.

Lines 41 and 42 create a 2-ms delay. This is to ensure that the LCD can process the data at its input before we present any new information to the LCD; see Table 6-2.

As this is the last instruction in this subroutine, the micro then goes back to the lcdOut subroutine as this is where this subroutine was called from.

The micro will now carry out the instruction on line 49 which calls the subroutine sendInfo () a second time and the above sequence repeats. However, as the bits in lcdTempInfo are again swapped, it will be the low nibble of the information that is sent to the LCD.

In this way all 8 bits of the information can be sent to the LCD in two 4-bit nibbles.

The microprocessor will now return to the lcdOut subroutine, but as it will have now completed all its instructions, it will now return back to the main loop via the lcdSetUp() subroutine.

This process is involved, and it uses what is termed "Nested Subroutines." You should be aware that there is a limit as to how many subroutines can be nested together in this way. This is restricted by what is termed "The Stack." So be careful when nesting subroutines like this.

One other important thing to remember about nested subroutines is that if a subroutine is to call another subroutine, the other subroutine must be written into the editing window before the subroutine that calls it. This is why the sendinfo subroutine is written before the lcdout subroutine as the lcdout subroutine will call the sendinfo subroutine.

Now we are back in the main loop, and the next line, line 108, calls another subroutine called writeString ("Hello World").

Note that this time, the brackets associated with this call are not empty. This is because this subroutine is expecting parameters to be sent down to it. This subroutine is one that has not been written by me but one that is termed "open source," and it is freely available for programmers to use. It basically creates a variable length array which the micro goes through one at a time to get information which on line 84 I have loaded into my variable lcdInfo.

Then on line 85, I call the subroutine lcdOut which sends the contents of lcdInfo to the LCD.

Note that the lettering inside the normal bracket of the subroutine call on line 108 is orange when viewed in MPLABX. This is because MPLABX uses colors to help distinguish different types of data. What actually happens with the orange text is that the ASCII character number for each character starting with 'H', in this case, is sent to the array. This is all done in the background by the compiler software. Note that to use this open source subroutine, you must include the stdio.h header file. This is done with the #include <stdio.h> in the program.

Note that on line 106, I create the forever loop as I don't want the micro to carry out all the above instructions again. Inside this loop, I send the characters 5, 7, and 9 out to the LCD; this is just to try and show you how numbers are sent to the LCD. Note that the ASCII for 5 is 0b00110101. The high nibble 0011 or 3 in hexadecimal. This puts us in the third column of the ASCII character table shown in Table 6-1. This is the column where the ASCII for the numbers 0 to 9 are listed and a few more. The numbers start at 0000 to 1001 which is the binary for 0 to 9. Therefore, to display a number 0 to 9, you simply set the high nibble to 0011 or 0X3 and use the low nibble to express what number you want to display, that is, 0000 to 1001 or 0X0 to 0X9.

I know the above description is very wordy, but it is quite difficult to explain in words how a program works. I hope I have gone someway toward explaining how the program and the instructions control and use the LCD. It is very important to be able to use the LCD. Of course, you could simply use the instructions without reading the explanation, but I feel it is important to understand how the instructions work.

# The New Aspects to PIC Programming in This LCD Program

There are some new aspects of PIC programming that I have introduced in this example, and I want to try and explain what they do.

## Arrays

This is a method by which you can create a list of variables and store them in locations one after the other. Then use them sequentially one at a time or randomly. It is very important to appreciate that the memory locations are set up one after the other in order. The array can store a variable using all the common data types, that is, unsigned char, integer, float, etc. To create an array, you simply declare it using the data type you want to use, then give it a sensible name followed by the '[6] ' square bracket. Inside the square bracket, you state how many memory locations you want to place in your array. When the compiler program compiles the program, it will place the start of the array in a memory location and then create the total number of memory locations immediately after the start location, one after the other. There are two arrays used in the LCD program above, and line 21 is where the first one is created char str[80]. This creates an array, named 'str', of 80 memory locations long in which data type char, 8 bits long using B7 to indicate the sign, positive or negative, of the number are stored.

At line 22 I have declared the second array. It is of data type unsigned char, and it has 8 locations. This is where I will store the 8 instructions to set up the LCD in the order that I want to use them. Note that by declaring the array as follows, unsigned char lcdInitialise [8] = , I have stated, by using the '=' sign, that I will define what should be stored in those 8 memory locations at the same time as declaring the array. That is why there is the ';' semicolon at the end of the defining curly bracket; the whole sequence of text is a program instruction. Try removing the ';' semicolon, and see what happens.

There is a comma after each statement of what is stored in this array. This is because this is a list, not a set of instructions; therefore, don't use the semicolon.

You can access the data in this array in two ways, one using a pointer, which is explained in the next section of the book, or one by calling the array in a similar way to calling a subroutine, but the array is not a subroutine, as follows:

lcdInfo = lcdInitialise [4] will pull up the contents of location 4 in the array and place a copy of it in lcdInfo. Note that the number of the first location in the array is always '0', so location [4] is the fifth item in the array.

# Using Pointers

Pointers can be used to point to locations inside an array. To create a pointer, it is best to create an array then create the pointer with the same name and type as the array. This is best explained by going through some example instructions as shown in the following.

Unsigned char dataStore [10]; // This creates an array of 10 locations one after the other, each being 8-bit memory locations.

Unsigned char *dataPointer; this creates a memory location that can be loaded with the particular address of a location in the dataStore array.

The array and pointer have now been created. The next step is to load the pointer with the address of the first memory location in the array. This is done with the following instruction:

```
dataPointer = dataStore;  //This will load the dataPointer with
                            the address of where the first
                            memory location of the dataStore
                            array is in memory. This means that
                            the dataPointer is now pointing to
                            the first location in the dataStore
                            array.
```

Now we can load some variables with the contents of the array using the following instructions:

```
Data0 = *dataPointer;    //This loads the variable Data0 with
                            the contents of the memory location
                            that dataPointer is pointing to.
                            In this case it is pointing to the
                            first location in the dataStore
                            array

dataPointer++;          //This increments the contents of
                            the dataPointer which means it now
                            points to the next location in the
                            dataStore array.

Data1 = *dataPointer;    // This loads Data1 with the contents
                            of the next memory location  in the
                            dataStore array.

dataPointer++;          //This increments the contents of
                            the dataPointer which means it now
                            points to the next location in the
                            dataStore array.
```

# Connecting the LCD in 8-Bit Mode

If the programmer has sufficient I/O, then they can use the LCD in 8-bit mode. This would have the main advantage of saving an extra visit to memory to get the full information to display on the LCD and save having to call the sendInfo subroutine twice.

The main differences are explained in Listing 6-2.

*Listing 6-2.*  Using the LCD in 8-Bit Mode

```
1.    //some definitions for some instructions
2.    #define firstbyte     0b00110011      //define the binary
                                              for first byte
3.    #define secondbyte    0b00110011      //define the binary
                                              for second byte
4.    #define lines2bits8  0b00111100      //define the binary
                                              for lines2bits8
5.    #define eightBitOp    0b00111000      //define the binary
                                              for eightBitOp
6.    #define twoLines      0b00101100      //define the binary
                                              for twoLines
7.    #define incPosition   0b00000110      //define the binary
                                              for incPosition
8.    #define cursorNoBlink    0b00001100   //define the binary
                                              for cusorNoBlink
9.    #define clearScreen  0b00000001      //define the binary
                                              for clearScreen
10.   #define returnHome   0b00000010      //define the binary
                                              for returnHome
11.   #define lineTwo      0b11000000      //define the binary
                                              for lineTwo
12.   #define doBlink      0b00001111      //define the binary
                                              for doBlink
```

165

```
13.   #define shiftLeft    0b00010000    //define the binary
                                             for shiftLeft
14.   #define shiftRight   0b00010100    //define the binary
                                             for
15.                                      shiftRight
16.   #define lcdPort      PORTB         //define which PORT
                                             LCD is connected to
17.   #define eBit         PORTAbits.RA0 //define which bit
                                             the LCD eBit is
                                             connected to
18.   #define RSpin        PORTAbits.RA1 //define which bit
                                             the LCD RSpin is
                                             connected to
19.   //some variables set up memory locations for the
         following variables
20.   unsigned char lcdInfo, lcdTempInfo, rsLine;
21.   unsigned char n;
22.   char lcdInitialis [7] =      //set up an array with 7
                                      memory locations and load
                                      the memory locations
                                      with the following LCD
                                      instructions
23.   {                           //opening curly bracket of
                                      array setup
24.   firstbyte,                    //the first instruction
25.   secondbyte,                   //the second instruction
                                      which is a copy of the
                                      first
26.   lines2bits8,                  //the instruction to use
                                      2 lines of characters
                                      and set up for 8 bit
                                      operation not 4 bit
```

27.    incPosition,                    //Instruction to make the
                                        cursor move one place
                                        to right after each
                                        data has been displayed
                                        on LCD

28.    doBlink,                .       //instruction to make
                                        cursor blink in current
                                        position

29.    clearScreen,                    //instruction to clear
                                        all data from LCD
                                        display

30.    returnHome,                     //instruction to send
                                        back to first position
                                        on line 1 of LCD

31.    };              //end of array brackets. Note the
                           semi colon is needed as the whole
                           sequence is a program instruction.

32.    //some subroutine these one line comments helps split the
         program up

33.    void lcdOut ()                  //start of lcdOut
                                        subroutine

34.    {                               //opening curly bracket
                                        of lcdOut subroutine

35.    lcdPort = lcdInfo;              //send info to LCD

36.    eBit = 1;                       //set eBit to logic '1'

37.    eBit = 0;                       //set eBit to logic '0'
                                        These two make the
                                        LCD aware that new
                                        information has come to
                                        its input pins.

| | |
|---|---|
| 38. | `TMRO = 0; while (TMRO < 15);` | //this is a 1.92mS delay at 7812.5Hz |
| 39. | `}` | //closing curly bracket of lcdOut subroutine |
| 40. | `void setUpTheLCD ()` | //start of subroutine to set up the LCD |
| 41. | `{` | //opening curly bracket of setUp subroutine |
| 42. | `TMRO = 0;` | //set TMRO back to 0 |
| 43. | `while (TMRO < 255);` | //wait until TMRO has reached 255 an initial 32.6ms delay before sending any info to lcd |
| 44. | `RSpin = 0;` | //set RSpin to logic '0' to tell LCD information coming is an instruction |
| 45. | `n = 0;` | //set the variable 'n' to 0 ready next loop |
| 46. | `while (n < 7)` | //set up while loop for sending instructions to LCD |
| 47. | `{` | //opening curly bracket for LCD loop |
| 48. | `lcdInfo = lcdInitialis [n];` | //load variable lcdInfo with first instruction in array lcdInitialis |
| 49. | `lcdOut ();` | //call subroutine lcdOut to send instruction to LCD |

```
50.   n ++;                    //add 1 to value of 'n'
                               ready to get next
                               instruction if n is less
                               than 7
51.   }                        //closing curly bracket for
                               LCD loop
52.   RSpin = 1;               //set RSpin back to logic
                               '1' as next information to
                               go to LCD will most likely
                               be data to be displayed
53.   }                        //closing curly bracket for
                               LCD loop
54.   void line2 ()            //start of subroutine to
                               send cursor to start of
                               line 2 on LCD
55.   {                        //opening curly bracket for
                               line2 loop
56.   RSpin = 0;               //set RSpin to logic '0'
                               to tell LCD information
                               coming is an instruction
57.   lcdInfo = lineTwo;       //Load variable lcdInfo
                               with instruction to go to
                               lineTwo
58.   lcdOut ();               //call lcdOut subroutine to
                               send instruction to LCD
59.   RSpin = 1;               //set RSpin back to logic
                               '1' as next information to
                               go to LCD will most likely
                               be data to be displayed
60.   }                        //closing curly bracket for
                               line2 loop
```

```
61.    void writeString
       (const char *words)
```
//this is subroutine that will display a whole string of characters on the display.

```
62.    {
```
//opening curly bracket for writeString loop

```
63.    while (*words)
```
// while the *words pointer is not pointing to the NULL char do what is inside the curly brackets

```
64.    {
65.    lcdInfo = *words;
```
//load what the *words pointer is pointing to into the variable lcdInfo

```
66.    lcdOut ();
```
//call the subroutine to pass the Info to the LCD

```
67.    *words ++;
```
//increment the contents of the pointer so that it is pointing to the next char in the array

```
68.    }
```
//closing bracket of the while loop

```
69.    }
```
//closing curly bracket for writeString loop

```
70.    void clearTheScreen ()
```
//This is a subroutine that clears all data from the display and sends the cursor back to start of screen

```
71.   {                          //opening curly bracket
                                  for clearTheScreen loop
72.   RSpin = 0;                  //set RSpin to logic
                                  '0' to tell LCD
                                  information coming is
                                  an instruction
73.   lcdInfo = clearScreen;      //Copy the data for
                                  clearScreen instruction
                                  into lcdInfo
74.   lcdOut ();                  //call the lcdOut
                                  subroutine to send
                                  instruction to LCD
75.   lcdInfo = returnHome;       //Copy the data for
                                  returnHome instruction
                                  into lcdInfo
76.   lcdOut ();                  //call the lcdOut
                                  subroutine to send
                                  instruction to LCD
77.   RSpin = 1;                  //set RSpin back to logic
                                  '1' as next information
                                  to go to LCD will most
                                  likely be data to be
                                  displayed
78.   }                          //closing curly bracket
                                  for clearTheScreen loop
79.   void main ()               //The main program loop
80.   {                          //opening curly bracket
                                  for main loop
81.   PORTA = 0;                 //Turn all outputs off
82.   PORTB = 0;
83.   PORTC = 0;
84.   PORTD = 0;
```

```
85.    TRISA = 0X00;          //make all of PORTA
                                 outputs
86.    TRISB = 0x00;          //make all of PORTB
                                 outputs
87.    TRISC = 0x00;          //make all of PORTC
                                 outputs
88.    TRISD = 0x00;          //make all of PORTD
                                 outputs
89.    ADCON0 = 0x00;         //turns off the adc
90.    ADCON1 = 0x0F;         //sets all bits to
                                 digital mode
91.    OSCTUNE = 0b10000000;  //this just sets the 8MHz
                                 as source for 31.25kHz
92.    OSCCON = 0b01110000;   //this selects the
                                 internal 8MHz frequency
                                 uses the primary osc as
                                 clock source
93.    T0CON = 0b11000111;    //this enables TMR0, sets
                                 it as 8 bit and max
                                 divide giving a clock
                                 tick of 128us
94.    setUpTheLCD ();        //This calls the
                                 subroutine to
                                 setUpTheLCD
95.    clearTheScreen ();     //This calls the
                                 subroutine to
                                 clearTheScreen
96.    while (1)              //This is the forever
                                 loop so that lines 81
                                 to 96 are only carried
                                 out once
```

```
97.   {                                    //This is the opening
                                             curly bracket for the
                                             forever loop
98.   writeString ("Working 8Bit LCD");    //This calls the
                                             writeString
                                             subroutine with
                                             the phrase
                                             Working 8Bit LCD
99.   line2 ();                            //This calls the
                                             subroutine to move the
                                             cursor to the start of
                                             line 2 on the LCD
100.  lcdInfo = 0x33;                      //This loads the variable
                                             lcdInfo with the ASCII
                                             for the number 3.
101.  lcdOut ();                           //This calls the
                                             subroutine to send the
                                             data in lcdInfo to the
                                             LCD
102.  while (1);                           //This for ever loop just
                                             makes the program halt
                                             at this point and there
                                             are no instructions in
                                             this loop. Note this is a
                                             one line instruction and
                                             there are no instructions
                                             before the end of
                                             instruction terminator
                                             the semi-colon.
```

103.  }                        //closing bracket of
                               the first while (1)
                               loop

104.  }                        //closing bracket of
                               the main loop

With the 8-bit operating mode of the LCD, there is no need to swap the nibbles of the data or instruction before sending it to the LCD. This approach uses two more I/O as well as the eight outputs for the data to the LCD. The two extra I/O are for the RSPIN and the EPIN of the LCD. Overall the approach may be simpler but you do need the extra I/O pins.

The circuit layout for the 8-bit LCD is shown in Figure 6-2.

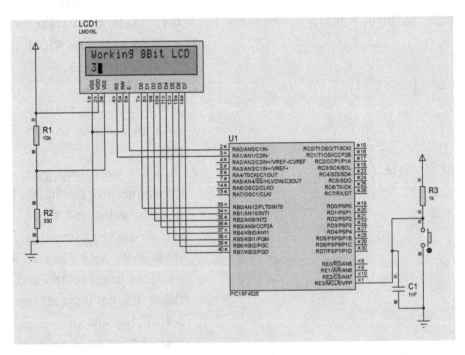

***Figure 6-2.*** *The 8-Bit LCD Circuit Note RA0 Is Connected to the EPIN and RA1 the RSPIN*

# The Volt Meter Program

In this extension of the previous program, we are going to combine the ADC with the use of the LCD. We are going to use the ADC to measure a variable voltage across a resistor and display the voltage on the LCD. This program will use the sprintf function that is freely available for us to use. It is a function that has been written as open source so that we can use it to display a floating point-type variable on any type of display.

## The Algorithm

The program will make use of the ADC to convert an analogue input on PORTA RA0 to a digital value.

- It will convert this value to represent a voltage from 0v to 5v.

- It will then use the 4-bit LCD program and the sprintf function to display the voltage measured on the LCD screen.

- It will constantly measure the voltage at the input.

- It will need one input PORTA RA0.

- It will need eight outputs to connect to the LCD. This will be via PORTB.

The program is shown in Listing 6-3.

*Listing 6-3.* The Volt Meter Program

```
1.    //some definitions
2.    #define firstbyte      0b00110011
3.    #define secondbyte     0b00110011
```

```
4.    #define fourBitOp     0b00110010    //this sets the
                                            LCD up for 4
                                            bit operation
                                            instead of 8 bit

5.    #define twoLines      0b00101100    //This sets the
                                            LCD to 2 lines
                                            mode

6.    #define incPosition   0b00000110    //This tells the
                                            LCD to increment
                                            the cursor
                                            position after
                                            any data is
                                            displayed

7.    #define cursorNoBlink 0b00001100    //this turns the
                                            cursor off so
                                            we don't see it
                                            flashing

8.    #define clearScreen   0b00000001    //this clears the
                                            screen of all
                                            display

9.    #define returnHome    0b00000010    //this sends the
                                            cursor back to
                                            start position
                                            on the display

10.   #define lineTwo       0b11000000    //this will send
                                            the cursor to
                                            the start of
                                            line 2 on the
                                            display

11.   #define doBlink       0b00001111    //this turns the
                                            cursor on and
                                            makes it blink.
```

```
12.    #define shiftLeft      0b00010000      //this shifts
                                               the cursor one
                                               position to the
                                               left
13.    #define shiftRight     0b00010100      //this shifts
                                               the cursor one
                                               position to the
                                               right
14.    #define lcdPort        PORTB           //this sets which
                                               port the LCD is
                                               connected to
15.    #define eBit           PORTBbits.RB5      //this sets
                                                  the bit for
                                                  the E pin on
                                                  the LCD
16.    #define rspin          PORTBbits.RB4      //this sets
                                                  the bit for
                                                  the RS pin
                                                  on the LCD
17.    //some variables
18.    unsigned char lcdData, lcdTempData, rsLine;
19.    unsigned char n;
20.    char str[80];
21.    float sysVoltage;
22.    //the subroutine

23.    void initialiseThePic ()
24.    {
25.    PORTA = 0;
26.    PORTB = 0;
27.    PORTC = 0;
28.    PORTD = 0;
```

```
29.    TRISA = OXff;
30.    TRISB = 0x00;
31.    TRISC = 0x00;
32.    TRISD = 0x00;
33.    ADCON0 = 0b00000001;    //bit 0 = '1' means adc on
                                bits 5,4,3&2 = '0' means
                                channel 0 AN0 is selected
34.    ADCON1 = 0b00001011;    //bits A0 to A3 are analogue
                                rest are digital
35.    ADCON2 = 0b00010001;    //select left justify 4TAD
                                Clock = FOSC/8 i.e 1MHz
                                TAD = 1uS
36.    OSCTUNE = 0x00;
37.    OSCCON = 0x74;          //this sets the internal
                                oscillator to 8MHz stable
38.    T0CON = OXC7;           //this turns timer 0 on,
                                makes it an 8 bit timer
                                with the maximum divide
                                rate

39.    }
40.    char lcdInitialise [8] =  //This creates a array 8
                                locations long and loads
                                each location with the
                                following data

41.    {
42.    firstbyte,
43.    secondbyte,
44.    fourBitOp,
45.    twoLines,
46.    incPosition,
47.    cursorNoBlink,
```

```
48.    clearScreen,
49.    returnHome,
50.    };
51.    void sendData ()
52.    {
53.    lcdTempData = (lcdTempData << 4 | lcdTempData >>4);
                    //this will swop the nibbles around in
                        lcdTempData ready to send to the LCD
54.    lcdData = lcdTempData & 0x0F;       // this basically
                                              ignores the last
                                              four bits of the
                                              lcdTempData
55.    lcdData = lcdData | rsLine;         // this allows us
                                              to determine if
                                              the info is an
                                              instruction or data
56.    lcdPort = lcdData;                  // this sends the info
                                              to the LCD
57.    eBit = 1;                           //These next two
                                              instructions are to
                                              tell the LCD new
                                              data has arrived and
                                              it should deal with
                                              it.
58.    eBit = 0;
59.    TMRO = 0; while (TMRO < 20);        //this is a 2.56mS
                                              delay at 7812.5Hz
60.    }
61.    void lcdOut ()
62.    {
63.    lcdTempData = lcdData;       // store the information in a
                                      temporary location
```

```
64.    sendData ();                          //this sends the
                                               high nibble of the
                                               information to the
                                               LCD

65.    sendData ();                          //this sends the
                                               low nibble of the
                                               information to the
                                               LCD

66.    }
67.    void setUpTheLCD ()
68.    {
69.    TMR0 = 0; while (TMR0 <255);          //a 32ms delay
70.    n = 0;                                 //This makes the
                                               variable 'n' = 0
                                               ready for the while
                                               loop at line 72

71.    rsLine = 0x00;                         // this ensures bit 4
                                               or the RS pin will be
                                               logic '0' as these
                                               are instructions

72.    while (n < 8)                          //whilst 'n' is less
                                               than 8 do what is
                                               inside the curly
                                               brackets.

73.    {
74.    lcdData = lcdInitialise [n];    //Load the variable lcdData
                                         with particular contents
                                         of the memory location in
                                         the array lcdInitialise
                                         the pointer is currently
                                         pointing to.
```

```
75.   lcdOut ();            //send that information to
                            the LCD.

76.   n ++;
77.   }
78.   rsLine = 0x10;        //this ensures bit 4 of the
                            rsLIne is a logic '1' for
                            data

79.   }
80.   void line2 ()
81.   {
82.   rsLine = 0x00;        // this ensures bit 4 or the
                            RS pin will be logic '0' as
                            these are instructions

83.   lcdData = lineTwo;
84.   lcdOut ();
85.   rsLine = 0x10;;       //this ensures bit 4 of the
                            rsLIne is a logic '1' for
                            data

86.   }
87.   void clearTheScreen () //This creates the subroutine
                            cleaTheScreen

88.   {
89.   rsLine = 0x00;        // this ensures bit 4 or the
                            RS pin will be logic '0' as
                            these are instructions

90.   lcdData = clearScreen; //this loads the variable
                            lcdData with the
                            instruction to clear the
                            screen

91.   lcdOut ();            //This sends the instruction
                            to the LCD
```

```
92.    lcdData = returnHome;          //this loads the variable
                                       lcdData with the
                                       instruction to return
                                       the cursor to the home
                                       position.
93.    lcdOut ();                     //This sends the instruction
                                       to the LCD
94.    rsLine = 0x10;                 //this ensures bit 4 of the
                                       rsLIne is a logic '1' for
                                       data

95.    }
96.    void gohome ()                 //This creates the
                                       subroutine gohome

97.    {
98.    rsLine = 0x00;                 // this ensures bit 4 or the
                                       RS pin will be logic '0'
                                       as these are instructions

99.    lcdData = returnHome;          //this loads the variable
                                       lcdData with the
                                       instruction to return
                                       the cursor to the home
                                       position.
100.   lcdOut ();                     //This sends the instruction
                                       to the LCD
101.   rsLine = 0x10;                 //this ensures bit 4 of the
                                       rsLIne is a logic '1' for
                                       data

102.   }
103.   void writeString (const char *words)
104.   {
```

```
105.  while (*words)          // while the *words pointer
                              is not pointing to the NULL
                              char do what is inside the
                              curly brackets
106.  {
107.  lcdData = *words;       //load what the *words pointer
                              is pointing to into the
                              variable lcdData
108.  lcdOut ();             // call the subroutine to pass
                              the data to the LCD
109.  *words ++;             // increment the contents of
                              the pointer so that it is
                              pointing to the next char in
                              the array
110.  }
111.  }
112.  void systemVoltage ()   //This creates a subroutine to
                              use the ADC to measure the
                              voltage
113.  {
114.  ADCONobits.GODONE = 1;  //This starts an ADC process
115.  while (ADCONobits.GODONE);   //This waits till the ADC
                                   has finished
116.  sysVoltage = (ADRESH*0.01953+ (ADRESL >>6)*0.0049);
                              //This converts the binary
                              value from the ADC to the
                              actual voltage.
117.  }
118.  void displayVoltage(float dp)    //This creates a
                                       subroutine to
                                       display the voltage
                                       on the LCD
```

```
119.  {
120.  sprintf(str, "%.2f", dp);    //This use the function
                                    sprintf to display the
                                    floating point value using
                                    2 decimal points
121.  writeString(str);            //This calls the writeSring
                                    subroutine to send the value
                                    to the LCD
122.  writeString(" Volts");       //This calls the writeSring
                                    subroutine to send the word
                                    Volts to the LCD
123.  }
124.  //The main program
125.  void main ()
126.  {
127.  initialiseThePic ();         //This calls the
                                    subroutine to initialise
                                    the PIC
128.  setUpTheLCD ();              //This calls the
                                    subroutine to set up the
                                    LCD
129.  while (1)                    This is a for ever loop
130.  {
131.  writeString ("The Voltage is");   // this sends the
                                        string "the voltage
                                        is" to the LCD
132.  line2 ();                    // call the subroutine line2
                                    to move the cursor to the
                                    beginning of line two on
                                    the LCD
```

```
133.  systemVoltage ();              //This calls the subroutine
                                       systemVoltage to go and
                                       measure the voltage
134.  displayVoltage (sysVoltage);//This calls the subroutine
                                       displayVoltage to display
                                       the voltage on the LCD
135.  gohome ();                    //This calls the subroutine
                                       gohome to send the cursor
                                       on the LCD back to the home
                                       position.
136.  }
137.  }
```

## The New Aspects of the Program

The following sections highlight some of the new aspects of the program via three new subroutines.

## The gohome Subroutine

```
1.    void gohome ()                 //This creates the
                                       subroutine gohome

2.    {
3.    rsLine = 0x00;                 // this ensures bit 4 or the
                                       RS pin will be logic '0' as
                                       these are instructions

4.    lcdData = returnHome;          //this loads the variable
                                       lcdData with the
                                       instruction to return
                                       the cursor to the home
                                       position.
```

5.    lcdOut ();                     //This sends the instruction to the LCD

6.    rsLine = 0x10;                 //this ensures bit 4 of the rsLIne is a logic '1' for data

## The sysVoltage Subroutine

1.    void systemVoltage ()      // This subroutine starts a conversion and stores the result into a variable called sysVoltage. Note sysVoltage must be of type float as it will be a decimal number

2.    {                          //opening curly brackets of the systemVoltage subroutine

3.    ADCONObits.GODONE = 1;     //This starts the ADC conversion by setting bit 1 of  ADCONO

4.    while (ADCONObits.GODONE);   //This waits for bit 1 of the ADCONO register to go to logic'0' This happens automatically when the conversion ends

5.    sysVoltage = (ADRESH*0.01953 + (ADRESL >>6)*0.0049);      //this line is explained below.

6.    }                           //closing curly brackets of the systemVoltage subroutine

Line 5 is used to convert the 10-bit result of the ADC conversion into an actual voltage reading. Firstly, you should remember that the 10 bit is split into an 8-bit number and a 2-bit number. Using left justification, the 8 bit is stored in the ADRESH register, and the other 2 bits are stored in bit 7 and bit 6 of the ADRESL register; see Figure 5-1. The 8 bits in the ADRESH have a resolution of 19.53mV, whereas the 2 bits in the ADRESL register have a resolution of 4.9mV; that is why both binary values have been multiplied as shown. However, before the 2 bits in the ADRESL register can be multiplied, they must be shifted 6 places to the right to move bit6 to bit0 and bit7 to bit1; that is why there is the symbol " >>6". In this way, you can use all 10 bits of the ADC instead of just the 8 bits in the ADRESH. This makes the result much more accurate.

It should be pointed out that the variable sysVoltage must be declared as a float in the variable declarations.

## The displayVoltage Subroutine

1.   void displayVoltage(float dp)          //This subroutine uses
                                             the sprinf function to
                                             display the contents of
                                             a float onto the LCD
                                             display
2.   {                          //opening curly brackets of the displayVoltage
                                 subroutine
3.   sprintf(str, "%.2f", dp);          //This calls the sprintf
                                        function with the float
                                        that has been passed down
                                        to the subroutine
4.   writeString(str);                  //This sends the result of
                                        the spintf function, str,
                                        to the display by calling
                                        the writeString subroutine

5.   `writeString(" Volts");`                //This calls the writeString
                                            subroutine to display the
                                            word Volts with a space
                                            before it

6.   `}`                      //closing curly brackets of the
                              displayVoltage subroutine

**NB:** To use the sprintf function, we must include the library that this function is written in. This is in the stdio.h header file. This means we must have the following include instruction as shown here:

`#include < stdio.h>`

This is added with the other include files and all the configuration words as is with all projects.

## Changing the Main Part of the Program

I have created a subroutine called initialiseThePic. This is just another way of making sure we only run these instructions once as we only call this subroutine once. However, you must make sure the calling of this subroutine is the first thing your program does.

1.   `while (1)`            //the forever loop
2.   `{`                    //opening curly brackets of the while (1)
3.   `writeString ("the voltage is");`       // this sends the
                                            string "the voltage
                                            is" to the LCD

4.   `line2 ();`                      // call the subroutine line2
                                      to move the cursor to the
                                      beginning of line two on the
                                      LCD

5.    systemVoltage ();          //This calls the subroutine
                                 systemVoltage where the adc
                                 is started and the result
                                 is store in the variable
                                 sysVoltage

6.    displayVoltage (sysVoltage); //This calls the subroutine
                                   displayVoltage and passes
                                   the variable sysVoltge to it

7.    gohome ();                 //This calls the subroutine to
                                 send the   LCD cursor back to
                                 the beginning of the display

8.    }                          //closing curly brackets of the while (1)

Figure 6-3 is the PROTEUS circuit with the PIC measuring and
displaying the voltage.

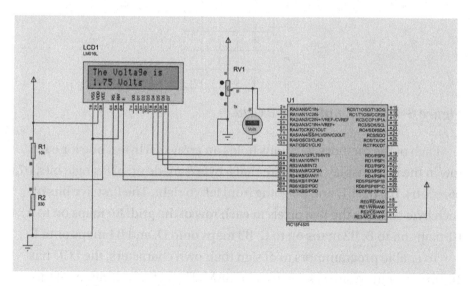

*Figure 6-3.*  *The Proteus Simulation*

# Creating Special Characters on the LCD

This program works on the concept that the LCD displays the different characters by turning on and off different pixels in a grid of pixels. The size of the pixel grid depends on the resolution of the LCD display. The resolution of the LCD in this exercise can be either 5 by 8 or 5 by 16 depending on whether or not we use 2 rows of 16 characters or 1 row of 16 characters on the LCD display. For our programs, we will use 2 rows of 16 characters; therefore, the resolution of each character is a 5 by 8 grid. The empty grid is shown in Figure 6-4.

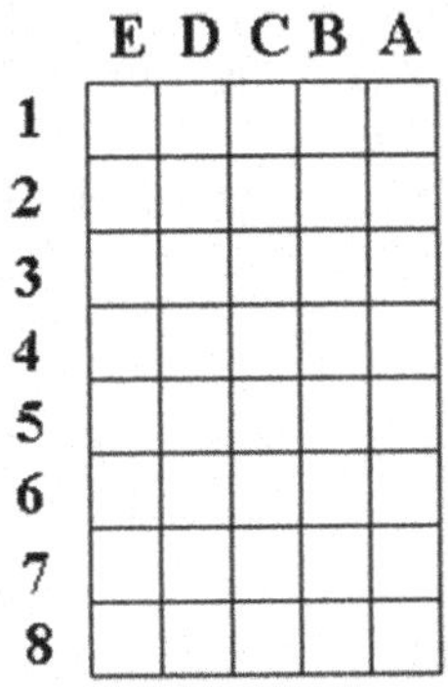

*Figure 6-4.* *The Empty 5-by-8 Grid*

Each of the memory locations holds an array of 8 bytes, one for each row in the LCD display grid. Note that a byte is made up of 8 single bits, b7, b6, b5, b4, b3, b2, b1, and b0 going from left to right. The first five bits of each byte controls the five pixels in each row of the grid. B0 maps on to A, B1 maps on to B, B2 maps on to C, B3 maps onto D, and B4 maps onto E.

To enable programmers to design their own characters, the LCD has 16 empty memory areas known as CGRAM. The actual addresses of this memory area are 00000000 to 00001111.

The programmer can write their own 8 bytes to be stored in these memory areas. However, to do this, the programmer must send an instruction to the LCD to tell it that we want to write data to be stored in this area. The 8-bit binary code for this instruction is 0b01000000 or 0X40. This is an instruction that the next information that follows is to be written into the first area of the CGRAM. There must now follow 8 bytes of data, and the first five bits of each byte defines which pixel will be turned on or off; a logic '1' means turn on the pixel, and logic '0' means turn the pixel off. There must be 8 bytes as with a resolution of 5 by 8, there will be 8 bytes in each memory area. When the eighth byte has been sent, the LCD will automatically open up the next area of the CGRAM. The LCD will now expect another 8 bytes of data until it has been told you have finished writing to the CGRAM.

To tell the LCD you have finished writing to the CGRAM, you must send the following instruction: 0b10000000 or 0X80. Note that the codes 0X40 and 0X80 are instructions and the LCD has to be put into that mode, whereas the following 8 bytes after the 0X40 instruction are data and the LCD must be put into that mode.

To try and help appreciate how the 8 bytes can define the pixel map for one special character, the following 8 bytes can be used to define the special character shown in Figure 6-5.

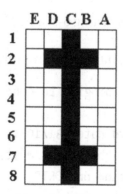

***Figure 6-5.*** *The Pixel Map for a Special Character to Display on the LCD*

The bytes are shown in Table 6-3.

***Table 6-3.*** *The 8 Bytes for Pixel Map Shown in Figure 6-5*

| ROW | B7 | B6 | B5 | B4 | B3 | B2 | B1 | B0 |
|-----|----|----|----|----|----|----|----|----|
|     |    |    |    | E  | D  | C  | B  | A  |
| 1   | 0  | 0  | 0  | 0  | 0  | 1  | 0  | 0  |
| 2   | 0  | 0  | 0  | 0  | 1  | 1  | 1  | 0  |
| 3   | 0  | 0  | 0  | 0  | 0  | 1  | 0  | 0  |
| 4   | 0  | 0  | 0  | 0  | 0  | 1  | 0  | 0  |
| 5   | 0  | 0  | 0  | 0  | 0  | 1  | 0  | 0  |
| 6   | 0  | 0  | 0  | 0  | 0  | 1  | 0  | 0  |
| 7   | 0  | 0  | 0  | 0  | 1  | 1  | 1  | 0  |
| 8   | 0  | 0  | 0  | 0  | 0  | 1  | 0  | 0  |

I hope this example goes someway to explaining how you can create some special characters to display on the LCD. To complete the explanation, I will write a program to display a series of special characters on the LCD.

The program is shown in Listing 6-4.

***Listing 6-4.*** The Special Characters Program

```
1.    //*This is a basic program to control the LCD using the
      PIC 18F4525
2.    Written by H H Ward dated 31/10/15.
3.    It is for use with the matrix multimedia prototype board
4.    using 4 bit operation on PORTB
5.    Extended to include creating special characters 27/03/16*/
6.    //some definitions
```

7.    #define firstbyte        0b00110011    // The first
                                             instruction to be
                                             sent to the LCD

8.    #define secondbyte       0b00110011    // The second
                                             instruction to be
                                             sent to the LCD

9.    #define fourBitOp        0b00110010    // Instruction to put
                                             the LCD into 4 bit
                                             data mode

10.   #define twoLines         0b00101100    //Instruction to set
                                             the LCD into 2 lines
                                             of characters

11.   #define incPosition      0b00000110    //Instruction to make
                                             LCD to automatically
                                             move the cursor one
                                             position after
                                             displaying a
                                             character

12.   #define cursorNoBlink    0b00001100    //Instruction to make
                                             not show the cursor
                                             on the LCD

13.   #define clearScreen      0b00000001    //Instruction to make
                                             clear the contents
                                             of the display

14.   #define returnHome 0b00000010          //Instruction to make
                                             cursor to move to
                                             the start of the
                                             display

15.   #define lineTwo   0b11000000           //Instruction to make
                                             cursor go to start
                                             of line 2 on the
                                             display.

16.   #define doBlink   0b00001111      //Instruction to make
display the cursor
as a Blinking
rectangle on the
display.

17.   #define shiftLeft   0b00010000      //Instruction to send
the cursor one
place to the left.

18.   #define shiftRight   0b00010100      //Instruction to
send the cursor one
place to the right

19.   #define lcdPort   PORTB      //tells the compiler
the LCD is
connected t0 portB

20.   #define eBit   PORTBbits.RB5   //tells the compiler
the ebit is on bit5
of portb

21.   #define startButton   PORTAbits.RA0   //tells the compiler
the waitbutton is
on bit0 of porta

22.   //some variables this idea is to use comments to split
the program up into different sections.

23.   unsigned char lcdData, lcdTempData, rsLine;   //declare some
variables
as unsigned
char

24.   unsigned char n;      //declare some variables
as unsigned char

25.   //the subroutine

26.    char lcdInitialis [8] =          //This sets up an array
                                        of 8 memory locations
                                        and loads each location
                                        with one of the
                                        instructions to set up
                                        the LCD
27.    {                                //the opening bracket of the
                                        array
28.    firstbyte,
29.    secondbyte,
30.    fourBitOp,
31.    twoLines,
32.    incPosition,
33.    cursorNoBlink,
34.    clearScreen,
35.    returnHome,
36.    };                               //the closing bracket of
                                        the array
37.    void sendData ()                 // a subroutine to send data
                                        to the LCD
38.    {                                //the opening bracket of the
                                        subroutine
39.    lcdTempData = (lcdTempData <<4 | lcdTempData >>4);
           //this swaps the two nibbles around.
40.    lcdData = lcdTempData & 0x0F;    //this loads the variable
                                        lcdData with the swapped
                                        around data in lcdTempData
                                        but only with the first 4
                                        bits.

| | |
|---|---|
| 41. `lcdData = lcdData \| rsLine;` | `//this performs a logical OR with lcdData and rsLine this is the control what bit 4 of the lcdData is` |
| 42. `lcdPort = lcdData;` | `//send info to LCD` |
| 43. `eBit = 1;` | `//this sets the eBit to a logic '1'` |
| 44. `eBit = 0;` | `//this sets the eBit to a logic '0' done to tell the LCD it has some new data` |
| 45. `TMRO = 0; while (TMRO < 20);` | `//this is a 2.56mS delay at 7812.5Hz` |
| 46. `}` | `//closing bracket if the sendData subroutine` |
| 47. `void lcdOut ()` | `// a subroutine to manipulate the data in variable lcdOut` |
| 48. `{` | `//the opening bracket of the subroutine` |
| 49. `lcdTempData = lcdData;` | `//saves a copy of lcdData in lcdTempData` |
| 50. `sendData ();` | `//calls the subroutine send Data for first time` |
| 51. `sendData ();` | `//calls the subroutine send Data for second time` |
| 52. `}` | `//the closing bracket of the subroutine` |
| 53. `void setUpTheLCD ()` | `//sets up the subroutine to set Up the LCD` |

| | |
|---|---|
| 54.   { | //the opening bracket of the subroutine |
| 55.   rsLine = 0x00; | // this loads the variable rsLine with 0. This is done to make sure bit 4 is a logic '0' to tell the LCD the next information is an instruction. |
| 56.   n = 0; | //this loads 0 into the variable 'n' done to make sure the following while instruction starts with n = 0 |
| 57.   while (n < 8) | //sets up the while loop which is carried out 8 times |
| 58.   { | //opening bracket of the while loop |
| 59.   lcdData = lcdInitialis [n]; | //this loads variable lcdData with data from the lcdInitialis array. This will be the data in the first location in the array if n = 0 but it is controlled by the value of n |
| 60.   lcdOut (); | //this calls the subroutine lcdOut |

61.    n ++;                         //this adds 1 to the value of
                                       n to make sure we use the
                                       next location in the array
                                       lcdInitials unless n = 8

62.    }                            //this is the closing
                                       brackets of the while loop

63.    rsLine = 0x10;               //this loads the variable
                                       rsLine with 0x10. This
                                       makes sure but 4 is now a
                                       logic '1' ready to tell the
                                       LCD the next information
                                       will be data to be
                                       displayed.

64.    }                            //this is the closing
                                       bracket of the setUpTheLcd
                                       subroutine.

65.    void line2 ()                // a subroutine named line2.
                                       This is a routine to send
                                       the cursor to the beginning
                                       of line2 on the LCD

66.    {                            //the opening bracket of the
                                       subroutine

67.    rsLine = 0x00;               //load rsLine with 0 to make
                                       sure we tell the LCD the
                                       next information is an
                                       instruction.

68.    lcdData = lineTwo;           //loads the variable lcdData
                                       with the instruction to
                                       move cursor to beginning of
                                       line 2

69.   lcdOut ();                         //call the subroutine lcdOut
                                         to send the instruction to
                                         the LCD

70.   rsLine = 0x10;                     //load rsLine with 0b00010000
                                         to make sure we bit 4 is a
                                         logic '1'this will tell the
                                         LCD the next information is
                                         data to be display

71.   }                                  //the closing bracket of the
                                         subroutine

72.   void writeString
      (const char *words)                //a subroutine to send a
                                         string of characters to the
                                         LCD

73.   {                                  //the opening bracket of the
                                         subroutine

74.   while (*words)                     //the while instruction that
                                         states that while we are
                                         not at the end of the array
                                         pointed to be the pointer
                                         *words then do what is
                                         between the curly brackets.

75.   {                                  //the opening bracket of the
                                         while statement

76.   lcdData = *words;                  //load the variable lcdData
                                         with the contents of the
                                         array memory location
                                         the pointer 8words is
                                         pointing to.

77.   lcdOut ();                         //call the subroutine lcdOut
                                         to send the instruction to
                                         the LCD

78.   *words ++;                           //increment the pointer
                                           *words to ensure it is now
                                           pointing to the next memory
                                           location in the array
                                           words.

79.   }                                    //the closing  bracket of the
                                           while statement

80.   }                                    //the closing bracket of the
                                           subroutine

81.   char firstCharacter [8] =            //this sets up an array of
                                           8 locations and loads each
                                           location with the data to
                                           create the pixel map for
                                           the character shown above
                                           in Figure 6-5

82.   {                                    //the following 8 bytes are
                                           the data for the character
                                           in Figure 6-5

83.   0b00000100,
84.   0b00001110,
85.   0b00000100,
86.   0b00000100,
87.   0b00000100,
88.   0b00000100,
89.   0b00001110,
90.   0b00000100,
91.   };
92.   char secondCharacter [8] =           //this sets up an array of
                                           8 locations and loads each
                                           location with the data to
                                           create the pixel map for
                                           the next character

```
93.   {
94.   0b00010101,
95.   0b00010101,
96.   0b00010101,
97.   0b00010101,
98.   0b00010101,
99.   0b00010101,
100.  0b00010001,
101.  0b00010001,
102.  };
103.  char thirdCharacter [8] =        //this sets up an array
                                       of 8 locations and
                                       loads each location
                                       with the data to create
                                       the pixel map for the
                                       next character

104.  {
105.  0b00000001,
106.  0b00000001,
107.  0b00000001,
108.  0b00000011,
109.  0b00000011,
110.  0b00000011,
111.  0b00000011,
112.  0b00000011,
113.  };
114.  char fourthCharacter [8] =       //this sets up an array
                                       of 8 locations and
                                       loads each location
                                       with the data to create
                                       the pixel map for the
                                       next character
```

```
115.  {
116.  0b00010001,
117.  0b00010001,
118.  0b00000100,
119.  0b00000100,
120.  0b00011011,
121.  0b00011011,
122.  0b00011111,
123.  0b00001110,
124.  };
125.  void clearTheScreen ()          //a subroutine to get the
                                        LCd to clear the acreen

126.  {
127.  rsLine = 0x00;                  //instruction mode
128.  lcdData = clearScreen;          //load the variable lcdDat
                                        with the instruction to
                                        clear the screen
129.  lcdOut ();                      //send the instruction to
                                        the LCD
130.  lcdData = returnHome;           //instruction to send the
                                        cursor to the beginning
                                        of the screen

131.  lcdOut ();
132.  rsLine = 0x10;                  //data mode
133.  }
134.  void writeToGram ()             //this is a subroutine to
                                        write code to the CGram
                                        locations in the LCD

135.  {
```

```
136.  rsLine = 0x00;              // ready for instruction.
137.  lcdData = 0x40;             //tells the LCD to open the
                                    first address in CGRAM
                                    area ready for us to write
                                    data into them
138.  lcdOut ();                  //calls the subroutine to
                                    send info to LCD
139.  rsLine = 0x10;              // ready for data as we
                                    have finished sending
                                    instructions.
140.  n = 0;                      //load n with 0 ready for
                                    the following while loop
141.  while (n < 8)               //do the following whilst n
                                    is less than 8
142.  {
143.  lcdData = firstCharacter [n];       //loads lcdData with
                                           the data from the
                                           array identified by
                                           the variable 'n'
144.  lcdOut ();       //calls the subroutine to start sending the
                         information to the LCD
145.  n ++;            //increment the variable n so it is looking
                         at the next location in the array.
146.  }
147.  n = 0;                  //loads n with zero ready to send the
                               next character to the LCD
148.  while (n < 8)
149.  {
150.  lcdData = secondCharacter [n];
151.  lcdOut ();
152.  n ++;
153.  }
```

```
154.  n = 0;                    //loads n with zero ready to send
                                  the next character to the LCD
155.  while (n < 8)
156.  {
157.  lcdData = thirdCharacter [n];
158.  lcdOut ();
159.  n ++;
160.  }
161.  n = 0;                    //loads n with zero ready to send
                                  the next character to the LCD
162.  while (n < 8)
163.  {
164.  lcdData = fourthCharacter [n];
165.  lcdOut ();
166.  n ++;
167.  }
168.  rsLine = 0x00;           //get ready for instruction
169.  lcdData = 0x80;          //command to go to DDRAM address
170.  lcdOut ();
171.  rsLine = 0x10;           //ready for data
172.  }
173.  void main ()            //the start of the main loop
174.  {
175.  PORTA = 0;             //the following 4 instructions loads 0
                                into the 4 ports just to make sure they
                                are not turning anything on
176.  PORTB = 0;
177.  PORTC = 0;
178.  PORTD = 0;
179.  TRISA = 0Xff;          // loads logic '1' to all bits in TRISA
                                thus making all porta inputs
```

```
180.   TRISB = 0x00;    // loads logic '0' to all bits in TRISB
                            thus making all portb outputs
181.   TRISC = 0x00;    // loads logic '0' to all bits in TRISC
                            thus making all portc outputs
182.   TRISD = 0x00;    // loads logic '0' to all bits in TRISD
                            thus making all portd outputs
183.   ADCON0 = 0x00;   //turns off the adc
184.   ADCON1 = 0x0F;   //sets all bits to digital mode
185.   OSCTUNE = 0b10000000;        //this just sets the 8MHz as
                                       source for 31.25kHz
186.   OSCCON = 0b01110100;         //this selects the internal
                                       8MHz frequency stable uses
                                       the primary osc as clock
                                       source
187.   T0CON = 0b11000111;          //this enables TMR0, sets
                                       it as 8 bit and max divide
                                       giving T812.5Hz therefore
                                       128usec per tic
188.   TMR0 = 0;                    //this load 0 into the TMR0
                                       register to ensure we start
                                       counting from 0
189.   while (TMR0 < 255);          //whilst TMR0 is less that
                                       255 do nothing. This is an
                                       initial 32.6ms delay before
                                       sending any info to lcd
190.   setUpTheLCD ();              //call the setUpTheLCD
                                       subroutine.
191.   clearTheScreen ();           //call the subroutine to
                                       clear the screen and send
                                       cursor back to start of the
                                       display.
```

192.  writeToGram ();                      //call the subroutine to
                                           write the data for the
                                           special characters to the
                                           Gram of the LCD

193.  while (!startButton);                //make the program wait until
                                           the start button on porta
                                           has been pressed and so
                                           gone to a logic '1'

194.  while (1)                            //set up the forever loop so
                                           that the PIC does not do
                                           the previous instructions
                                           again.

195.  {                                    //opening bracket of the
                                           forever loop

196.  writeString ("Special Chars");          //calls the subroutine
                                              writeString and sends
                                              the string Special
                                              Chars to be displayed
                                              on the LCD

197.  lcdData = 0x31;                      //this loads the variable
                                           lcdData with value 0x31
                                           this is the ASCII for the
                                           number 1.

198.  lcdOut ();                           //sends the data to the LCD
199.  lcdData = 0x32;                      //this loads the variable
                                           lcdData with value 0x32
                                           this is the ASCII for the
                                           number 2.

200.  lcdOut ();

```
201.  lcdData = 0x33;            //this loads the variable
                                   lcdData with value 0x33
                                   this is the ASCII for the
                                   number 3.

202.  lcdOut ();
203.  line2 ();                  //calls the subroutine to move
                                   the cursor to beginning of
                                   line 2 on the LCD display

204.  lcdOut ();
205.  lcdData = 0x00;            //this loads the variable
                                   lcdData with the value 0
                                   this is the address of the
                                   first area in the CGram of
                                   the LCD.

206.  lcdOut ();
207.  lcdData = 0x01;            //this loads the variable
                                   lcdData with the value 1
                                   this is the address of the
                                   second area in the CGram of
                                   the LCD.

208.  lcdOut ();
209.  lcdData = 0x02;            //this loads the variable
                                   lcdData with the value 2
                                   this is the address of the
                                   third area in the CGram of
                                   the LCD.

210.  lcdOut ();
211.  lcdData = 0x03;            //this loads the variable
                                   lcdData with the value 3
                                   this is the address of the
                                   fourth area in the CGram of
                                   the LCD.
```

```
212.  lcdOut ();
213.  lcdData = 0x20;                 //this loads the variable
                                        lcdData with the ASCII for
                                        the space see Table 6-1

214.  lcdOut ();
215.  lcdData = 0x48;                 //this loads the variable
                                        lcdData with the ASCII for
                                        capital H see Table 6-1

216.  lcdOut ();
217.  lcdData = 0x2E;                 //this loads the variable
                                        lcdData with the ASCII
                                        for the full stop, see
                                        Table 6-1.

218.  lcdOut ();
219.  lcdData = 0x57;                 //this loads the variable
                                        lcdData with the ASCII for
                                        capital W

220.  lcdOut ();
221.  lcdData = 0x2E;                 //this loads the variable
                                        lcdData with the ASCII for
                                        the full stop.

222.  lcdOut ();
223.  rsLine = 0x00;                  //sets the variable rsLine to
                                        0 ready to tell the LCD the
                                        next info is an instruction

224.  lcdData = returnHome;           //loads the variable lcdData
                                        with the instruction to
                                        return the cursor back to
                                        the beginning of the LCD

225.  lcdOut ();
```

```
226.  rsLine = 0x10;            //sets the variable rsLine
                                  to 1 ready to tell the LCD
                                  the next info is data to be
                                  displayed
227.  }                         //the closing brackets of the forever loop
228.  }                         //the closing brackets of the main loop
```

This program should help reinforce the principle that when we send information to the LCD, we are actually sending a number which represents the address of an area in the LCDs ram. Note that there are two areas of the LCDs ram that of the CGRAM where the user can store bytes that define the bytes of any special characters that the user wants to display. The other area of ram, the DDRAM, is where the manufacturers have stored the bytes for all the ASCII characters.

If you examine line 205 in Listing 6-4, you will see that we are loading the variable lcdData with the value 00000000 or 0x00. This is the address of the first area in the CGRAM where we have written the 8 bytes that define the pixel map for our first special character. Then in line 213, we load the value of 0010000 or 0x20. This is the address in the DDRAM where the manufacturer has stored the 8 bytes that define the pixel map for space or empty character. Again, it should be noted that the address in the DDRAM corresponds to the actual ASSCII character the memory area stores the pixel map data.

This is a very wordy description of how the LCD works and how we construct the 'C' commands to control the LCD. I think it is important that you understand how you construct your instructions and how you use them. By increasing your understanding, you will become a better programmer.

The array defined from lines 114 to 124 defines the map for the special character shown in Figure 6-6.

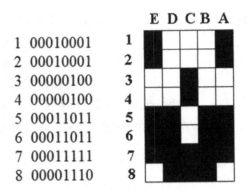

```
1 00010001    1
2 00010001    2
3 00000100    3
4 00000100    4
5 00011011    5
6 00011011    6
7 00011111    7
8 00001110    8
```

*Figure 6-6.* *The Character Map for My Face*

It should be noted that it is only the first 5 bits; b4, b3, b2, b1, and b0 and a logic '1' will turn the corresponding pixel on, whereas a logic '0' will turn it off. This concept is reinforced in Figure 6-6.

The simulation of this program is shown in Figure 6-7.

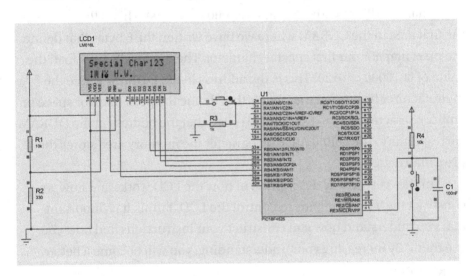

*Figure 6-7.* *The Special Characters Simulation*

# Summary

In this chapter we have studied how to set up the LCD and how to use the LCD to display the ASCII characters. We have also learnt how to display special characters that we can design ourselves.

We have also learnt how to use the ADC and use the sprint function to display the results of the ADC on the display.

The next chapter looks at the very useful concept of creating and using header files.

# CHAPTER 7

# Creating a Header File

This chapter covers how to create a header file. It then uses a header file in a program to control the LCD in 4-bit mode.

## Header Files

These can be used to reduce the size of a program listing and split a program up into different sections for different members of a team to work on. These header files will all be brought together using the #include statement in the main program.

One of the most useful applications of header files is when a lot of programs are going to use a peripheral device in **exactly** the same way in all the programs. One of the main peripheral devices we will use in our programs is the LCD screen. The approach would be to put the instructions for the LCD into a header file with the extension .h. Then include the header file in all the programs you want to use it in. You should realize that in all the programs; so far we have already used a header file; this is the xc.h file we have included in all our programs so far.

## Creating a Header File

To create a header file, we simply copy the instructions we want and place in a new file with the .h extension. You should give the header file a useful

© Hubert Henry Ward 2020
H. H. Ward, *C Programming for the PIC Microcontroller*,
https://doi.org/10.1007/978-1-4842-5525-4_7

name that explains what it is to be used for. The following will explain how
to create a header file using the instructions from the volt meter program
we have just created.

Make sure the project window with the project tree is visible as shown
in Figure 7-1.

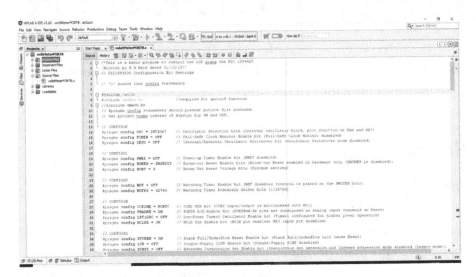

**Figure 7-1.** *The Main Screen with the Project Tree Visible*

If the project tree is not visible, then click on the "Window" option in
the main menu, and select the project option from the drop-down menu
that appears. You may have to move the window around the screen. This is
something you will have to practice as it is not my intention to explain how
to use every aspect of MPLABX; that is a book in itself.

With the project tree visible, right click on the Header File section
as shown in Figure 7-1. Then select new, and then select the "New xc8_
header.h" option. The window, as shown in Figure 7-2, should appear.

Give the file a suitable name that goes someway to describing what
the header file is for and give it the extension .h; you must give it the
correct extension. I have given it the name "LCD4bitOnPortb" as shown in
Figure 7-2.

214

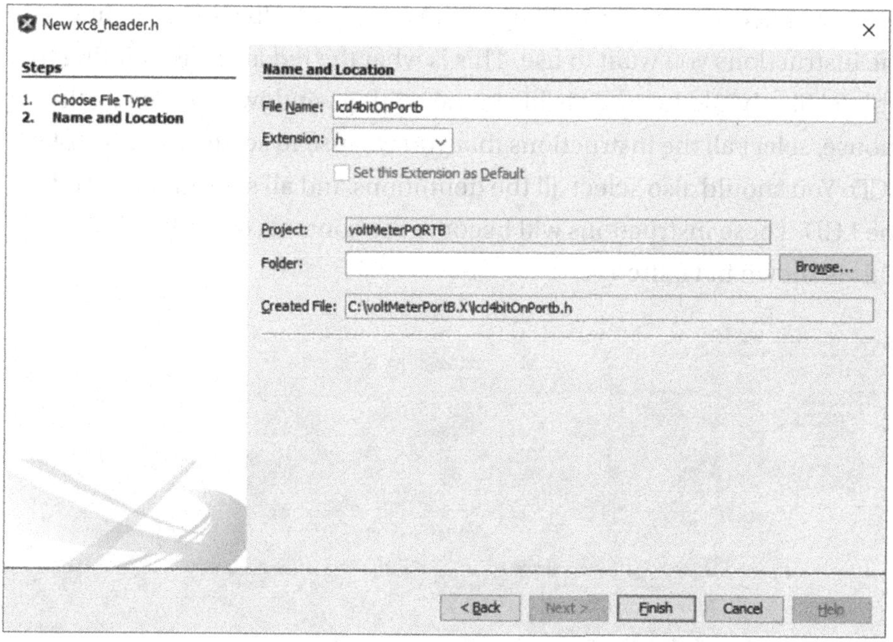

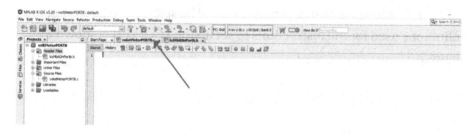

*Figure 7-2.* *The New Empty File Window for the Header File*

When you are happy with the file name, simply click finish, and you will be presented with the file ready for you to insert the instructions you want to put it in it. However, Microchip will have inserted a lot of text. I tend to delete all this so that I have an empty file. This is shown in Figure 7-3.

*Figure 7-3.* *The Header File Editing Window*

Now select the tab that will open the program 'c' file, which contains the instructions you want to use. This is what the red arrow is pointing to. This 'c' file should now be visible in the editing window. Now, using the mouse, select all the instructions that you will use to set up and control the LCD. You should also select all the definitions and all subroutines used for the LCD. These instructions will become the contents of the header file. This is shown in Figure 7-4.

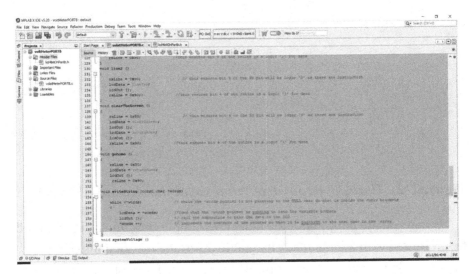

***Figure 7-4.*** *Selecting the Instructions to Copy into the Header File*

Note that the first instruction that should be selected is the start of the definitions used for the instructions to set up the LCD. This is shown in Figure 7-5.

**Figure 7-5.** *The Start of the Selection of the Instructions for the Header File*

Now that you have selected all the required instructions, cut all of them out of your program file. Then reopen the new header file, and paste the instructions into this file. You will need to save the contents of the new header file.

# Including the Header File into Your Program

Now that you have cut all the LCD instructions from the 'c' program file, we need to tell this 'c' file where it can find the newly created header file. There are two ways of doing this; one involves a local header file and the other involves a global header file.

A local header file is like the one we have just created. It is one that is saved inside the project we want to use it in, as with the current situation. To include this type of header file, all we need to do is add the following #include instruction to the compiler.

#include "LCD4bitOnPortb.h" You must write the quotation marks as shown.

Note that as you type the phrase "#include", the MPLABX software should recognize what you are doing and give you some suggestions of the file you may want to include, especially when you type the opening quotation mark. Your header file should be one of them.

I try to place all my include commands together; therefore, I will add this alongside the #include <xc.h> already in the 'c' file. Therefore, my 'c' file should look like that shown in Figure 7-6.

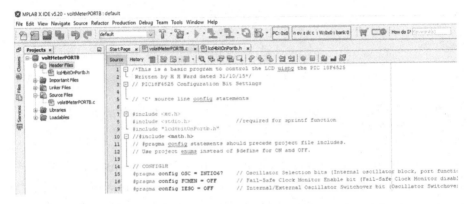

***Figure 7-6.*** *The Include Command for the New Header File*

I hope this clearly shows you how to create and include a local header file. If you now compile the project, it should compile without errors.

If your compilation throws up some errors, then go through the steps again carefully, and make sure you cut all the instructions for the LCD.

# The Global Header File

The more general way of using header files is to make them global. However, this will involve saving all the header files you create in the main include directory that the compiler software, which you are using, goes to find all the include files. If you do save them in the correct directory, then the header files will be available to all other projects you write. The path to where you should save your header files may be

```
C:\Program Files(x86)\Microchip\xc8\v1.32\include
```

or

```
C:\Program Files(x86)\Microchip\xc8\v2.10\pic\include
```

This may vary slightly, but you should be able to find the correct include directory.

If you save the header file this way, then to include them into your project you would have to write:

> #include <LCD4bitOnPortb.h> Note the use of the
> greater and less than symbols.

If you successfully save the file in the global location, you should be able to delete it from the local project directory. Having done so, it should still compile safely as the compiler program will successfully find the header file you want to include.

Having done this, you will now have a header file that should be globally available for all your projects.

# Creating a Header File for Your Configuration Instructions

The configuration words are instructions that allow us to set up the PIC in general terms. The main instruction is deciding where the PIC will get its primary oscillator source. There are a variety of options including a high-speed oscillator, HS, a lower-speed oscillator, XC, and RC oscillator and the internal oscillator block. Also, it can program the PIC to turn off the WDT and the LVP among many other aspects. In all the projects in this book, we will use the internal oscillator block and turn the WDT and the LVP off.

As long as you will do this for all your projects, you can create a header file for this configuration. Note: Give it a useful name that explains what it does, and save it in the global include directory.

I have done this for the rest of the projects I will use in this book. Open a new empty file under the Header Files in the project tree as before. The window shown in Figure 7-7 should open.

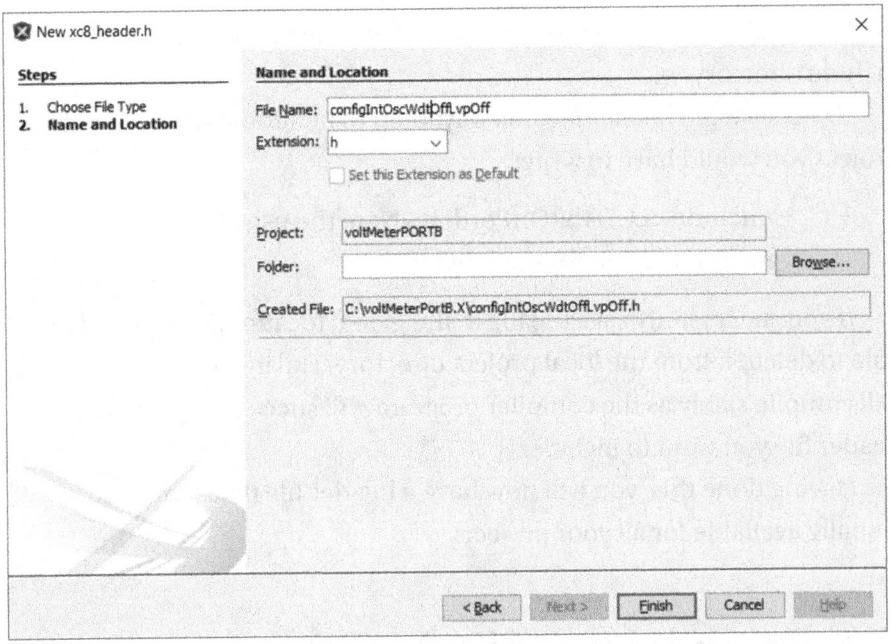

*Figure 7-7.* *The New Empty File Window*

Note I have chosen a very descriptive name for this header file conFigIntOscWdtOffLvpOff.h. Once you are happy with it, you should close the window by clicking finish. The editing window will open with the header file waiting to be written to. Simply paste in all the configuration instructions into the file, and save the file.

You should have now created a local header file for your configuration commands. If you save it in the global include directory, you will have a global header file for use in all the projects you want to configure the PIC in that same precise manner.

To include this global header file, we simply have to add the command:

```
#include <conFigIntOscWdtOffLvpOff.h>
```

The main 'c' program file is now much reduced, but you will have configured the PIC as you require.

# Summary

In this chapter we have studied header files. We have learnt what they are and how to create a global header file that can be used in all your projects.

In the next chapter, we will study a series of specific C programming commands. Then we will learn how to use one of the powerful debugging tools within MPLABX so that we can analyze what those programming commands do.

# CHAPTER 8

# Understanding Some Useful Code

This chapter involves some detailed analysis of the instructions. It will involve describing what the instruction should do and so predict the result of the instruction. It will then explain how you can single step through the program while watching the variables to see if the result is what we predicted. This chapter will also look at one of the very powerful debug facilities of the MPLABX IDE.

We will examine some of the main operations in 'C' code. The following is a list of the coding we will look at:

- Pointers; what they are and how to initialize them and how to use them

- The logical AND function, both individual bits and whole bytes. What is the difference and what they can be used for

- The simple increment and decrement

- The greater than and the less than

- A range of comparison instructions

After reading this chapter, you should have a good understanding of the above instructions and some possible application of the instruction. You will

© Hubert Henry Ward 2020
H. H. Ward, *C Programming for the PIC Microcontroller*,
https://doi.org/10.1007/978-1-4842-5525-4_8

also know how to use the debug tools in MPLABX to step through a program one instruction at a time and use a watch window to see what happens.

# The Trace Table

A good debugging method is used to create a trace table of what would be the result of the instructions in a program on all the SFRs and variables the program used. Then you would step through the instructions and monitor the SFRs and variables to check that the instructions worked as you thought. This chapter will give you a good insight to this powerful debugging technique.

# The Process

Listing 8-1 is the program used to discuss each instruction. We'll then go through each instruction's method of using the debug tools in MPLABX to check that our concepts are correct.

*Listing 8-1.* Sample Program

```
1.      unsigned char number1 = 0x0f, t, m, a, n, b;
                                    //this creates 6 8 bit
                                      memory locations but
                                      loads number1 with
                                      15 or 0b00001111
2.      int y = 2;                  //this creates a 16
                                      bit memory location;
                                      2 8 bits one after
                                      the other, called y
                                      and loads it with
                                      the value 2
```

3.      `int number2 = 0xffff, z;`          //this creates
                                            2 more 16 but
                                            locations and
                                            loads number2 with
                                            all logic '1's

4.      `float u = 2.55;`                   //this creates a
                                            variable 'u' that
                                            can store decimal
                                            numbers and loads
                                            it with 2.55

5.      `unsigned int number3 = 0xffff;`    //this creates a
                                            16 bit number,
                                            'number3' where
                                            all 16 bits are
                                            used for the value
                                            and loads it all
                                            logic '1's = 65535

6.      `unsigned char list [5];`           //this creates an
                                            array of 5 8 bit
                                            memory locations
                                            one after the
                                            other

7.      `unsigned char *listpointer;`       //this creates a
                                            16 bit memory
                                            location that can
                                            be used to store
                                            the address of a
                                            location in an
                                            array. This is
                                            16bits as it holds
                                            an address which
                                            is 16 bits long

| | | |
|---|---|---|
| 8. | `void main()` | //This is the main loop in the program |
| 9. | `{` | //the opening bracket for the main loop |
| 10. | `number1++;` | //this adds 1 to the value in number1 |
| 11. | `number1 = number1 + 2;` | //this makes number1 = itself but with 2 added to it |
| 12. | `number2 = number1 - 2;` | //this will load number 2 with what was in number 1 but takes 2 off it |
| 13. | `number2 = 0b1111111111110000;` | //this will change the value stored in number2 to -16 |
| 14. | `m = 0;` | //this loads m with 0 |
| 15. | `a = 0;` | //this loads a with 0 |
| 16. | `y = 5;` | //this loads y with 5 |
| 17. | `z = ++y;` | // 'y' is incremented first then z = what y has become |
| 18. | `z = y++;` | // z equal what y was then y is incremented |
| 19. | `z = (unsigned char) u;` | // z changes to an unsigned char to show all 8 bits which equal 251 in decimal. This is called "Casting" |
| 20. | `y = 7;` | //y is now set to 7 |

| 21. | y = ~y; | //this will simply invert all the bits in the variable 'y' |
|-----|---------|--------------------------------------------------------------|
| 22. | y = 7; | //this makes y = 7 |
| 23. | z = y<<1; | // z is back as an integer and its value is what was in y but shifted left one bit Y is unchanged |
| 24. | z = y>>1; | // z is what was in y but shifted right one bit but Y is unchanged Note with the shift right instruction the LSB is simply lost. With the shift left instruction the MSB is lost. |
| 25. | a = 0b00010011; | //this makes a = 19 |
| 26. | y=(a>0) ? a : -1; | // This a test. Is 'a' greater than 0. If the test is true then 'y' will = 'a'. If the test is Untrue then 'y' will = -1 |
| 27. | y=(a==0) ? a : -1; | // This a test. Is 'a' equal to 0. If the test is true then 'y' will = 'a'. If the test is Untrue then 'y' will = -1 |

28.      y=(a>0) ? z : -1;

// This a test. Is 'a' greater than 0. If the test is true then 'y' will = 'z'. If the test is Untrue then 'y' will = -1

29.      listpointer = list;

//this loads the pointer listpointer with the address of the first location in the list array

30.      *listpointer =2;

//this will load the first location in the list array with the value 2

31.      listpointer ++;

//this will increment the value in *listpointer. This means it will be pointing to the next location in the array list

32.      *listpointer = 5;

//this will load the second location in the array list with 5

33.      listpointer = list;

//this loads the pointer listpointer with the address of the first location in the array list

34.     `a = a & 0xF0;`                //this will force the
                                       first 4 bits of a to
                                       logic '0' and the last
                                       four bits will only be
                                       a logic '1' if the last
                                       four bits in 'a' are
                                       already a logic '1'

35.                                    // this is termed bit
                                       masking or bit testing,
                                       testing to see if a
                                       bit in a variable is a
                                       logic '1'

36.     `t = 5;`                       //this loads the
                                       variable t with the
                                       value '5'

37.     `if ( t && 7 == t)m = 5;`      //this tests to see if
                                       the value of 't' is
                                       the same as 7. If it
                                       is then m = 5 if it is
                                       not then m = 9. This
                                       is anding the byte

38.     `else m = 9;`                  //this is the else
                                       statement for the if
                                       then else instruction.
                                       Note you don't always
                                       need to write the else
                                       keyword but in this
                                       case we do need the
                                       else

39.     `n = 0b00001000;`              //this loads the value 8
                                       into the variable 'n'

40.     `if (n & 0b00001000)m = 5;`

| | | |
|---|---|---|
| 41. | `else m = 3;` | //this is a test to see if bit 3 of the variable 'n' is at a logic '1' if it is then m = 5, if its Not m = 3. This is bit anding |
| 42. | `if (n & 0b00000001)t = 4;` | |
| 43. | `else t = 2;` | //this is a test to see if bit 0 of the variable 'n' is at a logic '1' if it is then t = 4, if its not t = 2 |
| 44. | `n = 10;` | //This loads the variable 'n'with 10 |
| 45. | `for (a = 0, a < 5, a++;)` | //this creates a for do loop that goes through it 5 times |
| 46. | `{` | //opening bracket for the for do loop |
| 47. | `*listpointer = n;` | //this loads the current location that the listpointer is pointing to with the value that is in 'n' |
| 48. | `listpointer ++;` | //this increments the pointer listpointer so that it is pointing to the next location in the array |
| 49. | `n = n + 2;` | //this increases the value of n by 2 |

| 50. | `}` | `//the closing bracket of the for do loop` |
| 51. | `while (1);` | `//this is a for ever loop that forces the micro to stop at this instruction as it will do nothing forever` |
| 52. | `}` | `//the closing bracket of the main loop` |

# Lines 1–6

I am hoping that the comments for lines 1–6 do describe what the instructions will do. Just note that with some of the variables, we are loading them with an initial value as in line 1 "number1 = 0x0f"; this creates an 8 bit memory location and loads it with the initial value of 0x0f which is 15 in decimal.

# Line 7 unsigned char *listpointer;

In line 7 we are creating a pointer which is a variable that points to something. In this case we will make it point to a memory location in an array. This means that the 16-bit number in the pointer will be the actual address of one of the memory locations in the array. We will see this work later in the program. Note that the '*' is there to tell the compiler this is not a simple variable; it is a pointer.

Lines 8 and 9 are fairly straightforward, and the comments describe what they are.

# Line 10 number1++;

This will simply increase the value of number1 by 1. As number1 was loaded initially with 15, after this instruction, it will be 16.

# Line 11 number1 = number1 + 2;

If you want to increase the value of a variable by more than 1, it can be done this way. Therefore, this instruction will add 2 to the variable number1. After this instruction, the value stored in number1 will be 18.

# Line 12 number2 = number1 - 2;

This will change the value stored in number2, which was 32767, with 16. This is 2 less than the value stored in number1. Note also that the value on number1 will be unchanged.

I have not shown the instruction number2 --; as this will simply subtract 1 from the current value in number2.

# Line 13 number2 = 0b1111111111110000;

This changes the value that is in number2 from 16 to -16. This works because the MSB bit15 of number2 is not part of the value. It tells the compiler that the number is either positive, when bit 15 is a logic '0', or negative when bit 15 is a logic '1'. In this case, bit 15 is a logic '1', so the number is a negative number. However, to determine what the value is, the compiler must carry out a 2s compliment on the 16 bits in the instruction. In this way the binary value 0b1111111111110000 means -16. See the Appendix for an explanation of what 2s compliment is.

Lines 14 through 16 are fairly straightforward, and the comments describe what they are.

# Line 17 z = ++y;

This increments the value of 'y' by 1, making it 6, and then copies this value into 'z.' Therefore, after this instruction, both 'y' and 'z' will be 6.

# Line 18 z = y++;

This instruction makes 'z' the same value that is stored in 'y' and then increments the value of 'y'. Therefore, after this instruction, 'z' will again be 6, but 'y' will be 7.

# Line 19 z = (unsigned char) u;

This instruction changes the data type of the variable 'z.' This is called casting. Note that the change in type only lasts for this instruction. The data type for the variable 'u' is a float, and the value is 2.55. However, this is stored in 'z' as an unsigned char. This means the numbers after the decimal point will be lost. Therefore, after this instruction, the value in 'z' will be 2, not 2.55

Line 20 is a fairly straightforward, and the comments describe what it is.

# Line 21 y = ~y;

This instruction will simply invert all the bits in the variable. This means the bits that where logic '1' become logic '0' and what were logic '0' become logic '1.'

Therefore, before this instruction the bits in 'y' were

0000000000000111

After this instruction, they will be

233

1111111111111000. Note that this is will become -8 when the 2s compliment has finished. Note that 'y' is an int or integer which means the MSB is not part of the number.

Line 22 is a fairly straightforward, and the comments describe what it is. After this instruction, the value in 'y' will be 7.

# Line 23 z = y<<1;

This moves a copy of what is in 'y' into 'z,' but before the value is copied, the bits are shifted one bit to the right. The value in 'y' is in binary.

0000000000000111

Before this is copied into 'z,' the bits are shifted one place to the right. Therefore, the bits in 'z' will be

0000000000001110 which is 14. Note that shifting bits 1 bit to the left simply multiplies by 2. Moving the bits 1 bit to the right simply divides by 2.

Note that the value in 'y' is unchanged. The number of places the bits are shifted is specified by the value after the >>, in this case 1, but it could be 2, 3, 4, and so on.

# Line 24 z = y>>1;

This does a similar action as with line 23 but shifts the bits one place to the left before copying the value into 'z.'

The bits in 'z' will now be

0000000000000011 which is 3.

Note that the value in 'y' will be unchanged at 7.

Line 25 is fairly straightforward and the comments describe what it is. After this instruction, the value in 'a' will be 19.

# Line 26 y=(a>0) ? a : -1;

This is the first type of instruction with a bracket. When brackets are used, we are using a test, and the result of the test will either be true, a logic '1', or untrue a logic '0'. The expression inside the bracket is defining the test as "is 'a' greater than 0." In line 25 we set the value as 'a' to 19, and so it is greater than 0. This means the test is true, and so 'y' will become a copy of 'a'. Therefore, in this case the test is true, and after this instruction, 'y' will be 19 the same as 'a'.

If the test was found to be untrue, then 'y' would take on the other value stated in this instruction which in this case is -1.

# Line 27 y=(a==0) ? a : -1;

The test in this instruction is "is a equal to 0." Well the value stored in 'a' is still 19 which means the test is untrue, and so after this instruction, the value in 'y' will be -1. Note that the value in 'a' will be unchanged.

# Line 28 y=(a>0) ? z : -1;

The test is the same as that in line 26. The result is again true, but this time the variable 'y' will take on the value of that stored in 'z' and not 'a'. This means after this instruction, the value of 'y' will be 3 as this is what is stored in 'z' from before in the program.

# Line 29 listpointer = list;

This is the first instruction that uses the pointer listpointer. Note that I have given the pointer this name as the array that I will be using this to point to has been given the name list; see line 6 where I created the array list having 5 memory locations each 8-bit-long as they are to store unsigned chars.

This instruction loads the memory location listpointer with the first address of the array list. This means the listpointer is pointing to the first location in that array. Note that the variables window will most likely show the address of the first location in the array in hexadecimal format, for example, 0X13. This is the same as 19 in decimal or 0000000000010011 in binary. This is why you need to appreciate decimal, binary, and hexadecimal. These numbers systems are explained in the Appendix.

# Line 30 *listpointer =2;

This will load the memory location that the listpointer is pointing to with the value of 2. As with line 29, we made the listpointer point to the first location in the list array; then after this instruction, the value of the first location in the list array will have be 2. Remember that the first location in the array is location '0'.

# Line 31 listpointer ++;

This simply increases the value stored in the listpointer by 1. As the values in the pointer are the addresses inside the array list, then after this instruction, the listpointer will be pointing to the next location in the array list.

# Line 32 *listpointer = 5;

This will load the current memory location that the listpointer is pointing to with the value 5. Therefore, after this instruction, the first location in the array list will have the value 2 and the second will have the value 5.

# Line 33 listpointer = list;

This simply is a repeat of the instruction at line 29. After this instruction the contents of the listpointer will be the address of the first location in the array list.

This is to get the listpointer pointing to the first address in the array list ready for the for do loop at line 44.

# Line 34 a = a & 0xF0;

This is the first of a type of instruction termed bit masking or bit testing. This is actually bit masking where the idea is to mask out the first 4 bits, termed the low nibble. This works on the principle of the logic AND function where a '1' AND a '1' result in a logic '1'. However, a '1' AND a '0' produces a logic '0'.

This instruction uses the single '&' symbol which means this is a bit AND. With this type of instruction each, individual bit of the stated variable is ANDED with the data expressed in the instruction.

The data in the instruction is

0XF0 which in binary is 11110000

The data in the variable that the AND is ANDED with is

'a' which has the binary value of 00010011 which is 19. See line 25.

This means the first 4 bits in the variable 'a' will be masked out and result in 4 logic '0's as they will be ANDED with a logic '0'. The next four bits, the high nibble, bits 4, 5, 6, and 7, will be a copy of the four high bits in the variable 'a'.

Line 35 is just an extra set of comments.

Line36 simple loads t with the value of 5.

# Line 37 if ( t && 7 == t)m = 5;

This instruction combines the test with a bit instruction. However, the double '&&' sign means the ANDing is done on all 8 bits of the variable and data. This means the test "is the result of the full byte AND of the variable 't' with the value 7 the same as the value in 't'". If the test is true, then value of the variable 'm' will go to 5.

# Line 38 else m = 9;

This else is connected to the if instruction in line 37. We know what will happen if the results of the test are true. This else instruction tells us what will happen if the test is untrue. It the test is untrue, then the value of the variable 'm' will go to 9.

As 't' was loaded with 5 at line 36, then the test will be untrue, and so after this instruction, the value of 'm' will change to 9, because of the else statement on line 38.

An application of this type of instruction could be with entry to a room via a keypad. The result of a 4-digit number entered in via a keypad could be stored in the variable 't'. It could then be matched to a pre-stored 4-digit code using this type of instruction, and the door could be opened if the result is true or not if the result was untrue.

# Line 39 n = 0b00001000;

This is loading the variable 'n' with the number 8. It is really setting bit 4 to a logic '1'. This is ready for the next bit test in lines 40 and 41.

# Line 40 if (n & 0b00001000)m = 5;
# Line 41 else m = 3;

This is an individual bit test to see if bit 4 of the variable 'n' is a logic '1'. If it is, the test is true, and the value of m is set to 5. If bit 4 of the variable 'n' is not a logic '1', the test will be untrue, and the variable 'm' will be set to 3. Note that the value of the variable 'n' will remain unchanged. We know that the test will be true, and so after this instruction, the value of m will be 5.

# Line 42 if (n & 0b00000001)t = 4;
# Line 43 else t = 2;

This is the same type of test as described in lines 40 and 41 except that the bit that is being tested in line 42 is bit 0 of the variable 'n'. We know from before that bit 0 of the variable 'n' is a logic '0', not a logic '1'. This means that the test will be untrue. Therefore, after this instruction, the value of the variable 't' will be 2, not the 4 that it would have been if the result of the test was true.

# Line 44 n = 10;

This simply loads the variable 'n' with the value 10 ready for the next instructions.

# Line 45 for (a = 0, a < 5, a++;)

This sets up a for do loop that is carried out 5 times. The loop is described between the opening bracket at 45 and 50. The instructions inside the bracket, note that this is not a normal test bracket, firstly load the variable 'a' with the value 0. Then it carries out the test is 'a' less than 5, which it is. As the test is true, the micro will then carry out the instructions listed inside the curly brackets. Then the value of 'a' is incremented. The loop starts again until a = 5 and the test a < 5 becomes untrue. When it is untrue, the micro moves outside the loop.

Line 46 is simply the opening curly bracket of the for do loop.

## Line 47 *listpointer = n;

This loads the memory location that the listpointer is pointing to with the value stored in the variable 'n' which at this time is 10.

You should remember that in line 33, we made the pointer listpointer point to the first location in the array list. This then means after this instruction, the data in the first location of the array list will be 10.

## Line 48 listpointer ++;

With this instruction we simply increase the value stored in listpointer by 1. This means that the pointer listpointer will now be pointing to the second memory location in the array list.

## Line 49 n = n +2;

Now we simply add 2 to the value that is stored in the variable 'n'. Therefore, after this instruction, the values stored in the variable 'n' will be 12.

The micro will now go through the instructions of the for do loop another 4 times. In this way we can load the 5 memory locations in the array list with the data from Table 8-1.

*Table 8-1.* *The Contents of the Array List After the For Do Loop Has Finished*

| Location in List Array | Identifier for the Location | Value in The Location |
| --- | --- | --- |
| 1st | 0 | 10 |
| 2nd | 1 | 12 |
| 3rd | 2 | 14 |
| 4th | 3 | 16 |
| 5th | 4 | 18 |

This is quite a succinct way of filling the memory locations in an array with data. Note that arrays can have a large number of memory locations.

Line 50 is the closing bracket of the for do loop.

# Line 51 while (1);

This sets up a forever loop as the result of the test described in the bracket will always be true a logic '1'. This simply halts the program at this instruction as the micro will forever do nothing.

Line 52 is the closing bracket of the main loop.

# Debugging the Program

The best way to show how to use the debug tools in MPLABX is to go through the instructions of the program would and show them in a video. I have produced such a video that can be used to show the process. However, what I will do in this chapter is show some screenshots to show you the main points of the process.

# Compiling the Completed Program

After writing the complete program, the first thing to do is to build and run the program. To do this, click the mouse on the Debug Main Project icon in the main menu bar shown in Figure 8-1.

***Figure 8-1.***  *The Debug Main Project Icon*

This will build the program which tests the syntax of the program for errors, and assuming there are no errors, the program will be loaded into the PIC. If you have chosen the simulator as the tool as shown in Figure 2-6, then the simulated PIC will be loaded with the program. If you have downloaded the program to a practical PIC using the ICD3 or ICD4 can, the process will be the same. In this example, I have used the MPLABX simulator PIC

While the program compiles and the program is loaded to the PIC, the output window should be visible during this process. Once the program loads successfully, the screen should look something like what is shown in Figure 8-2.

CHAPTER 8   UNDERSTANDING SOME USEFUL CODE

***Figure 8-2.*** *The Completed Output Window*

The output window should be visible on the screen. You will see a small 'x' next to a small dot in the right-hand corner of the output window. If you click the mouse on the small dot, the window will now be fastened inside the editing area of the screen as shown in Figure 8-3.

***Figure 8-3.*** *The Output Window Now Moved into the Editing Area*

There will now be a small minimize icon in the right-hand corner of the output window. If you click on this, the output window will drop into the low menu bar at the bottom of the screen. The program is still running in the back ground. You should minimize the output window.

If you select the small 'x' instead of the small dot, the output window will disappear, but you can get it back by either hitting the control key and the number 4, Crtl4, together, or by selecting the word window from the main menu bar and selecting the word output from the drop-down menu bar that appears. I prefer to have the output window minimized to the bottom menu bar, as shown in Figure 8-4.

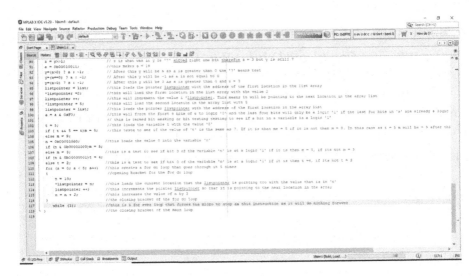

***Figure 8-4.*** *The Output Window Minimized*

Once you have placed the output window out of the way, we now need to select the variables that we want to look at as the program progresses. To do this select the word windows from the main menu bar, then select the word debugging from the drop-down menu, and select variables from the fly-out menu that appears as shown in Figure 8-5.

244

**Figure 8-5.** *The Variables Fly-Out Menu*

You could have selected the Watches window from the fly-out menu as there is not much difference between the two options; it is down to experience and personnel choice. Having selected the variables, the screen should look something like this shown in Figure 8-6.

**Figure 8-6.** *The Variables Window*

You may have to change the size of the window by selecting the boarders, and when the mouse changes to a double arrow, move the window accordingly.

Now we need to select what variables we want to look at. Really it should be all the variables we have created in the program. In other programs, you may want to be more selective. To select the variables, you want to simply click the mouse on the small blue diamond shape with the plus sign on it on the side menu in the variables window. An empty row should appear, and the small diamond that was grayed out should now be blue. Click the mouse on this now visible diamond, and the new watch window will appear. You should then click the mouse on the variable named 'a', then while holding the control key, select the names of all the other variables you want to look at. They should be highlighted blue as shown in Figure 8-7.

Note that the unsigned char number3 will not be visible in the new watch window. This is because this variable is not actually used in the program even though we have defined it and loaded it with 0XFFFF which 65535.

***Figure 8-7.*** *The New Watch Window*

Once you have selected all the variables you want to watch, simply click OK, and the variables will appear inside the variables window.

You can decide what type of information you want to display in the variable window by clicking the right-hand button on the mouse on any of the titled boxes at the top of the variable list. The fly-out menu will now be visible as shown in Figure 8-8. You should tick or un-tick the type of information you want displayed.

*Figure 8-8.* *The Variable Type Fly-Out menu*

You now need to pause and reset the program so that it will start at the first instruction. To do this click the mouse on the orange pause symbol on the menu bar. When this happens the blue circle with the two white arrows becomes visible. If you now click the mouse on this button, the program will reset, and the screen should now look like the one shown in Figure 8-9.

***Figure 8-9.*** *The Program Reset*

There should be the green highlighted instruction as shown in Figure 8-9. This should be the first instruction in the program. The IDE is now waiting for you to either run the program by pressing the green circle with the white arrow inside it, something we don't want to do this time, or get the program to single step through the instructions one at a time. This is what we want to do so that we can examine the variables as they change according to the instructions of the program. To do this we must click the mouse on the blue square with the curved orange arrow pointing down. The program will now step through the instructions of the program one at a time each time you press this button, but it will not step into the instructions of a function or subroutine.

Note that there is a blue square with a straight orange arrow pointing vertically down. This is to allow you to step into a function or subroutine if you want to.

Well I know it is not ideal trying to describe this process in a textbook, but I hope I have described it well enough for you to use this powerful

248

debug option in MPLABX. You should now step through each of the instructions and see if the results of the instructions agree with the analysis of the instructions in section.

You will need to take your time and maybe need to reread the description.

# Summary

I hope you have found this chapter useful and you have been able to step through the program. Understanding what the instructions actually do and how they work is very important to the programmer. Also being able to use the debugging tools of the IDE is essential to solving problems in a program. Both aspects will help you become a better programmer.

In this final chapter, we have studied some specific C programming instructions. We have also studied how to use one of the debugging tools within MPLABX to study the outcome of those instructions to confirm that they do what we expected them to do.

# APPENDIX

# Additional Resources

## Useful Definitions

Bit operators

| Operator | Description |
|----------|-------------|
| & | AND each bit |
| \| | OR each bit (inclusive OR) |
| ^ | EXOR each bit (exclusive OR) |
| <<n | Shift left n places |
| >>n | Shift right n places |
| ~ | One's compliment (invert each bit) |

For xample, if 'x' = 1111 1111, then:

| Operation | Result |
|-----------|--------|
| x & 0X0F | 0000 1111 |
| x \| 0X0F | 1111 1111 |
| x^0X0F | 1111 0000 |
| x = x<<2 | 1111 1100 |
| x = x>>4 | 0000 1111 |
| x = ~x | 0000 0000 |

© Hubert Henry Ward 2020
H. H. Ward, *C Programming for the PIC Microcontroller*,
https://doi.org/10.1007/978-1-4842-5525-4

# Mathematical and Logic Operators

| Operator | Description |
|---|---|
| + | Leaves the variable as it was |
| - | Creates the negative of the variable |
| ++ | Increments the variable by 1 |
| -- | Decrements the variable by 1 |
| * | Multiplies the two variables $y = a*b$ |
| / | Divides $y = a/b$ |
| % | Used to get the remainder of a division of two variables $m = a\%b$ |
| < | Less than if $(y < a)$ means y is less than a |
| <= | Less than or equal to if $(y < =a)$<br>means y is less than or equal to a |
| > | Greater than if $(y > a)$<br>means y is greater than a |
| >= | Greater than or equal to if $(y > =a)$<br>means y is greater than or equal to a |
| = | Makes the variable equal to $y = 3$<br>After this y takes on the value of 3 |
| ! | Not if (!PORTBbits.RB0) not bit0 of portb which means if bit0 of portb is logic 0 |
| && | Whole register AND |
| \|\| | Whole register OR |
| ? | This is a test operator $y=(a>0) ? a : -1$<br>This test to see if 'a' is greater than 0. If it is, then y becomes equal to 'a'; if it's not, then $y = -1$ |

# Keywords

| Keyword | What It Does |
|---|---|
| typedef | Allows the programmer to define any phrase to represent an existing type |
| #ifndef | This checks to see if a label you want to use has not been defined in any include files you want to use |
| | If it has, it does not allow you to define it now. If it hasn't, you are allowed to define it now |
| #define | You can define what your label means here |
| #endif | This denotes the end of your definition after the #ifndef code |
| sizeof | Returns the size in number of bytes of a variable |

Global variables are variables that once declared can be read from or written to anywhere from within the program.

# Data Types

| Type | Size | Minimum Value | Maximum Value |
|---|---|---|---|
| Char | 8 bits | -128 | 127 |
| unsigned char | 8 bits | 0 | 255 |
| int | 16 bits | -32,768 | 32,767 |
| unsigned int | 16 bits | 0 | 65,535 |
| short | 16 bits | -32,768 | 32,767 |
| unsigned short | 16 bits | 0 | 65,535 |
| short long | 24 bits | -8,388,608 | 8,388,607 |
| unsigned short long | 24 bits | 0 | 16,777,215 |

| Type | Size | Minimum Value | Maximum Value |
|------|------|---------------|---------------|
| long | 32 bits | -2,147,483,648 | 2,147.483,647 |
| unsigned long | 32 bits | 0 | 4,294,967,295 |
| Float | 32 bits | | |

Floating point numbers

| Type | Size | Min Exponent | Max Exponent | Min Normalized | Max Normalized |
|------|------|--------------|--------------|----------------|----------------|
| float | 32 | -126 | 128 | $2^{-126}$ | $2^{128}$ |
| Double | 32 | -126 | 128 | $2^{-126}$ | $2^{128}$ |

# Functions

Functions are similar to subroutines in that they are small sections of program code that are used to perform a specific function. They can be set up to return a particular type of variable, or they can be set up to return no variable.

Example

```
Char getvalue ()
```

This function will return a char value at the end of its instructions.

```
unsigned int age ()
{
}
```

This function will return an unsigned int value at the end of its instructions.

```
void motoron ()
{
}
```

This function will not return a value when it ends.

Functions, just like subroutines, have to be called from the main program. In 'C' this is done by stating the name of the function as follows:

```
getvalue ();
age ();
motoron ();
```

These will call the specified function.

Parameters

Some functions may require parameters that can be used within the function. This is true for both void and non-void functions. If a function needs a parameter that it will use within the function, it needs to be expressed when the function is declared. The following is an example of such a function:

```
void delay250 (char x)
    {
            while (x>0)
                {
                        TMR4 = 0;
                        while (TMR4<35211);
                        x--;
                }
    }
```

To call this function, use

```
delay250 (4);
```

This will assign the value 4 to the char 'x', and so this will create a total of a 1-second delay.

# Loops

All 'C' programs are a collection of loops. The loops will be carried out either once as in subroutines or for as long as their test condition is true. The most common loops are while loops. For example:

```
While (a == 1)
{
Do what is inside the curly brackets.
}
```

The test condition is that 'a' becomes equal to 1. While this test is true, that is, a is 1, then do what is inside the curly brackets.

# Numbering Systems Within Microprocessor-Based Systems

As will become evident in the study to come, microprocessor-based systems use the binary number system. This is because the binary number system can only have one of two digits, either a '0' or a '1'. These states have been called logic '0' or logic '1' as in electronic devices. Note also that all the logic operations such as AND, OR, NAND, NOR, NOT, and EXOR all work using binary format. The binary format can be used to mimic the logic states of "TRUE" or "FALSE" precisely; and best of all, they can be represented by voltage, that is, 0V for logic '0' and +5V for logic '1'.

Therefore, it is essential that the modern engineer gains a full understanding of the binary number system. This appendix is aimed at teaching the reader all they need to know about binary numbers.

# Binary Numbers

These are a series of '0s' and '1s' that represent numbers. With respect to microprocessor-based systems, the numbers they are representing are themselves representing codes for instructions and data used within microprocessor-based programs. We, as humans, cannot easily interpret binary numbers as we use the deanery number system. The deanery number system uses the base number 10 which means all the columns we put our digits in to form numbers are based on powers of 10. For example, the thousand column is based on $10^3$, and the hundreds column is based on $10^2$. The tens is on $10^1$ and the units is $10^0$. Try putting $10^0$ in on your calculator using the $x^y$ button, and you will find it equals 1; in fact, any number raised to the power 0 will equal 1.

# Converting Decimal to Binary

Probably the first step to understanding binary numbers is in creating them, that is, converting decimal to binary. There are numerous ways of doing this, but I feel that the most straightforward is to repeatedly divide the decimal number by 2, the base number of binary. This is shown here:

Example 1

Convert 66 to binary.

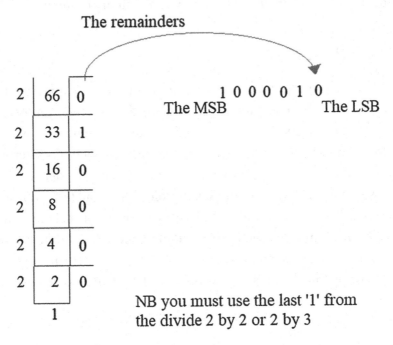

The remainders

| 2 | 66 | 0 |
| 2 | 33 | 1 |
| 2 | 16 | 0 |
| 2 | 8 | 0 |
| 2 | 4 | 0 |
| 2 | 2 | 0 |
| | 1 | |

1 0 0 0 0 1 0
The MSB          The LSB

NB you must use the last '1' from the divide 2 by 2 or 2 by 3

Simply keep on dividing the number by 2, putting the answer underneath as shown, with the remainder to the side. You should note that all the remainders are either **0** or **1**. These digits actually make up the binary number. Note also the last division always results in an answer '**1**'; we stop there, no more dividing.

To create the binary number, we take the top of the remainders, as shown, and put it into the least significant bit, or column, for the binary number. The other remainder digits follow on thus making up the complete 7-digit number.

Converting from Binary to Decimal

It would be useful to determine if the binary number shown does actually relate to 66 in decimal. This is done by converting back into decimal the binary number 1 0 0 0 0 1 0. To do this, we must realize that numbers are displayed in columns. The columns are based on the base number of the system used. With binary numbers, the base number is 2; therefore, the columns are based on powers of 2. This is shown in the following table:

| Base No. | $2^7$ | $2^6$ | $2^5$ | $2^4$ | $2^3$ | $2^2$ | $2^1$ | $2^0$ |
|---|---|---|---|---|---|---|---|---|
| Decimal Equivalent | 128 | 64 | 32 | 16 | 8 | 4 | 2 | 1 |
| Binary Number | | 1 | 0 | 0 | 0 | 0 | 1 | 0 |

To complete the conversion, we simply sum all the decimal equivalents where there is a 1 in the binary column.

In this case the sum is 64+2 = 66

Example 2

Convert 127 to binary and check the result.

**The remainders**

| 2 | 127 | 1 |
| 2 | 63 | 1 |
| 2 | 31 | 1 |
| 2 | 15 | 1 |
| 2 | 7 | 1 |
| 2 | 3 | 1 |
| | 1 | |

1 1 1 1 1 1 1
The MSB                    The LSB

NB you must use the last '1' from
the divide 2 by 2 or 2 by 3

| Base No. | $2^7$ | $2^6$ | $2^5$ | $2^4$ | $2^3$ | $2^2$ | $2^1$ | $2^0$ |
|---|---|---|---|---|---|---|---|---|
| Decimal Equivalent | 128 | 64 | 32 | 16 | 8 | 4 | 2 | 1 |
| Binary Number | 0 | 1 | 1 | 1 | 1 | 1 | 1 | 1 |

To complete the conversion, we simply sum all the decimal equivalents where there is a 1 in the binary column.

In this case the sum is: 64+32+16+8+4+2+1 = 127

Exercise 1

Covert the following numbers to binary, and check your results by converting back to decimal. **Show all workings out**.

99

255

137

# Adding and Subtracting Binary Numbers

Adding and subtracting numbers are perhaps the most basic operations we can carry out on numbers. Binary numbers follow the same rules as decimal, but there are only 2 allowable digits. Also, computers don't actually subtract numbers as the following will show.

Exercise 2

> Add the following decimal numbers in 8-bit binary notation. Note: Check your answers.
>
> 23+21, 35+123, 125+75
>
> Worked example
>
> Remember binary numbers have only two digits: '0' or '1'.
>
> Add 23 to 21 in 8-bit binary.

Method:

Convert to 8-bit binary, and add; remember the following four rules:

```
0+0 = 0
0+1 = 1
1+0 = 1
1+1 = 0 with 1 to carry
```

23 in 8 bit binary is

0 0 0 1 0 1 1 1 **note we must state all 8 bits as it is 8 bit binary.**

By the same process 21 in binary is  0 0 0 1 0 1 0 1

Therefore the sum is             0 0 0 1 0 1 1 1

+ 0 0 0 1 0 1 0 1

---

0 0 1 0 1 1 0 0

---

To check your answer, put the result into the lookup table, then add the decimal equivalent.

| Power | $2^7$ | $2^6$ | $2^5$ | $2^4$ | $2^3$ | $2^2$ | $2^1$ | $2^0$ |
|---|---|---|---|---|---|---|---|---|
| **Decimal Equivalent** | 128 | 64 | 32 | 16 | 8 | 4 | 2 | 1 |
| **Binary Number** | 0 | 0 | 1 | 0 | 1 | 1 | 0 | 0 |

Sum is 32 + 8 +4 = 44.

# Subtracting Binary Numbers

Exercise 3

Microprocessor-based systems actually subtract numbers using a method which is addition. This involves using the 2s compliment of a number, and it is best explained by the following example.

> Subtract the following decimal numbers using 8-bit binary 2s compliment; check your answers:
>
> 128 - 28, 79 - 78, 55 - 5, 251 - 151
>
> Worked example
>
> Convert the two numbers to binary using the method shown previously.
>
> 128 in 8-bit binary is 10000000. **NOTE that we MUST use ALL 8 bits**.
>
> 28 in 8-bit binary is 00011100.
>
> Take the 2s compliment of 00011100 as this is the number that we are subtracting from 128.

**Only create the 2s compliment of the subterand, the number we are subtracting with**.

NOTE: We must use a full 8-bit number putting extra 0 in where needed.

To take the 2s compliment, firstly take the compliment, and then add binary 1 to the compliment: the compliment of the binary number is found by simply flipping all the bits, that is, a '0' becomes a '1' and a '1' becomes a '0'.

```
Compliment of  00011100   is  1 1 1 0 0 0 1 1
add binary 1           +       0 0 0 0 0 0 0 1
                               _____

                               1 1 1 0 0 1 0 0
                               _____
```

Now add the 2s compliment to the first binary number as shown:

```
                          1 0 0 0 0 0 0 0
                      +   1 1 1 0 0 1 0 0
                          _____

result is                 0 1 1 0 0 1 0 0
                          _____
```

**NOTE: THE LAST CARRY INTO THE NINTH DIGIT IS DISCARDED AS THERE CAN ONLY BE THE SPECIFIED NUMBER OF DIGITS, 8 IN THIS CASE.** Don't forget we added 1 so we should give it back.

The binary result converts to 100 in decimal. This is the correct result. Check your answers in the usual way.

Note that computers subtract in this method because we can only create an adder circuit in logic.

# The Hexadecimal Number System

Microprocessor-based system can only recognize data that is in binary format. In its most basic form, this means that all data inputted at the keyboard should be in binary format. This is quite a formidable concept. Just think every letter of every word must be inputted as a binary number. It takes at least 4 binary digits to represent a letter, and so typing words into a computer would be very difficult indeed. Thankfully, word-processing programs take ASCII characters to represent the letters you press at the keyboard.

With the type of programs we will be writing into microcomputers, we will actually be typing in 2 characters to represent the codes for the instructions or data of the programs we will write. If we were to type these in as binary numbers, it would take 8 binary bits to make each code. This would be very time-consuming and difficult to make sure we get right. To make things easier, we will use the hexadecimal numbering system. This system has 16 unique digits which are

0  1  2  3  4  5  6  7  8  9

After this we cannot use 10 as this uses two digits: a 1 and a 0. Therefore, we must use 6 more unique digits. To do this. we use the first 6 letters of the alphabet. Therefore, the full 16 digits are

0  1  2  3  5  6  7  8  9 A B C D E F

Remember we are going to use the hexadecimal number to represent binary digits and this revolves round the idea that 1 hexadecimal digit represents 4 binary digits as the 4 binary bits in decimal go from 0 to 15, that is, 16 numbers. Therefore, every 8-bit binary number can be represented by 2 hexadecimal digits. This makes typing in the code for programs much quicker and more secure than using the full binary numbers that computers use. Note that to accommodate the user typing inputs as hexadecimal digits, there is a program in micro's ROM to convert the hexadecimal to binary for us. However, we will look at converting binary to hexadecimal.

Exercise 4

Convert the following 8-bit binary numbers to hexadecimal:

10011110, 10101010, 11111111, 11110000, 00001111, and 11001101

Worked example

Method: Split the 8 bits into two 4-bit numbers.
Convert each 4 bit into the decimal equivalent, then
look up the hexadecimal for the decimal equivalent
in the lookup table: **NOTE: Treat each four binary
bits as a separate binary number**.

```
Convert    1 0 0 1    |  1 1 1 0
           Dec   9    |    14
           Hex   9    |    E
Answer     10011110 in Hex is 9E
```

In this way 8-bit binary numbers can be converted into 2 hexadecimal
digits.

# Index

## A, B

Acquisition time
  8-Mhz oscillator, 129
  20-Mhz oscillator, 129, 130
ADC input channels
  algorithm, 132, 133
  instructions analysis, 134
  setup, 131
  simulation circuit, 134
  variable voltage, 132
ADCON0 control
    register, 120–122
ADCON1 register, 122, 123
ADCON2 control register
  ADC conversion, 125
  ADC operation
    timing, 127
  capacitor, 126
  conversion result, 124
  justification, 125
  Microchip, 126
  TAD periods, 127, 128
Analogue inputs, 119, 120
Analogue to Digital Converter
    (ADC), 33–36
Assembler language, 5

## C

Casting, 226, 233
Comments, 24, 27, 52
Complex instruction set chip
    (CISC), 2
'C' programming language, 5, 23

## D

Data mode, LCD controller
  analogue inputs, 140
  ASCII character set, 138, 139
  connection, 141
  RS pin, 141
  VEE pin, 141
Debug tools
  drop-down menu bar, 244
  editing area, 243
  fly-out menu, 244, 245, 247
  function/subroutine, 248, 249
  menu bar, 242
  MPLABX simulator PIC, 242
  new watch window, 246
  program reset, 248
  tick/un-tick information, 247
  variables window, 245, 246

© Hubert Henry Ward 2020
H. H. Ward, *C Programming for the PIC Microcontroller*,
https://doi.org/10.1007/978-1-4842-5525-4

# N

# O

# P, Q

Printed in the United States
by Baker & Taylor Publisher Services